# The Closing Battles of the Peninsular War

# The Closing Battles of the Peninsular War

## The British Army Under Wellington in the Pyrenees & South of France, 1813-14

ILLUSTRATED

The British Army Under Wellington

1813-1814

T. Miller Maguire

With an Introduction by Charles Oman

LEONAUR

*The Closing Battles of the Peninsular War*
*The British Army Under Wellington in the Pyrenees & South of France, 1813-14*
by T. Miller Maguire
With an Introduction by Charles Oman

ILLUSTRATED

First published under the title
*The British Army Under Wellington 1813-1814*

Leonaur is an imprint of Oakpast Ltd

Copyright in this form © 2021 Oakpast Ltd

ISBN: 978-1-78282-936-2 (hardcover)
ISBN: 978-1-78282-937-9 (softcover)

**http://www.leonaur.com**

Publisher's Notes

# Contents

# Preface

This little work is peculiar in one sense, inasmuch as the greater part of it is not the production of its author. It was really composed in great part by the general responsible for the operations of the British, Portuguese, and Spanish troops against Marshal Soult's army.

The Duke of Wellington was not only an illustrious commander, he was also a great diplomatist, a constant student of military history from his youth up, and a voluminous and able writer.

By the very kind permission of Mr. John Murray I was allowed to make lengthy quotations from the duke's *Despatches* in my articles in the *United Service Magazine*, of which this book is a reproduction.

T. Miller Maguire.

10, Earl's Court Square, S.W.
February 3rd, 1907.

FRANCE

Sebastian

Bayonne

Fuenterrabia

Durango

Roncevalles

Vitoria Pampeluna

Pyrenees Mts.

Calahorra

Figueras

Gerona

Tudelo

Rio Ebro

Saragossa

Lerida

Barcelona

Mts.

Siguenza

s of Somo Sierra

Tortosa

Tarragona

DRID

40

Ucles

Majorca

na

cid I

N

Murviedro

na R.

Valencia

Iviza

orena

s de la

lina

Castalla

Alicante

Murcia

C. Palos

Cartagena

anada

C. Gata

Map of the
SPANISH CAMPAIGN.

English Miles

0  20  40  60  80  100                    200

# Introduction on the Course of the War

By Charles Oman

In 1808 Bonaparte conceived the iniquitous idea of seizing the crown of Spain and substituting for its wretched King Charles IV. a monarch of his own choosing. Charles was an obedient ally, but he was so thoroughly incompetent that his assistance did not count for much: the emperor imagined that a nominee of his own would prove a more profitable helper. But the way in which he set about the conquest of Spain was characteristically treacherous and tortuous. He drafted a large army into the Peninsula under the excuse that he was about to attack Portugal, almost the last state in Europe which had not yet accepted the Continental System. Declaring that "the House of Braganza had ceased to reign," he poured his forces into Portugal, whose prince-regent fled overseas to Brazil without attempting to offer resistance. But while one French Army under General Junot had marched on Lisbon, large detachments followed behind, and occupied, under the guise of friends, the Spanish capital Madrid, and the fortresses of Barcelona, Pampeluna, and San Sebastian.

The Spaniards suspected no harm till Napoleon showed his hand by a disgraceful piece of kidnapping. King Charles IV. and his son, Prince Ferdinand, a worthless and useless pair, had been engaged in a bitter quarrel with each other. Bonaparte summoned them both to visit him at Bayonne, just across the French frontier, in order that he might arbitrate between them and heal their quarrel. They were foolish enough to obey this insolent mandate: when they arrived, however, he put them both in confinement, bullied them into signing an abdication, and sent them prisoners into France. He then took the astounding step of appointing his own brother Joseph Bonaparte as the successor of Charles IV., and the numerous French troops scattered through Spain everywhere proclaimed the usurper. The populace of Madrid rose, but was put down with ruthless severity, and Joseph made his appearance in the capital at the head of a strong guard.

Bonaparte had believed that centuries of misgovernment and disorganisation had so broken the spirit of the Spanish nation that his impudent and treacherous scheme could be carried to a successful end. He was soon undeceived: the Spaniards, in spite of the decay of their ancient power and wealth, and the incompetence of their rulers, still possessed a healthy sense of national pride: they were, moreover, the most obstinate, fanatical, and revengeful race in Europe. Though deprived of their princes, and confronted with French garrisons treacherously installed in their fortresses, they sprang to arms in every province. In most quarters their raw levies were easily beaten by the French veterans, but a series of fortunate chances enabled the insurgents of the South to surround and capture at Baylen an army under General Dupont, which had forced its way into Andalusia (July 20, 1808). This was the first serious check which the French arms had sustained since Napoleon had been proclaimed emperor, and it had important results. Joseph Bonaparte and his troops had to abandon Madrid, to retire beyond the Ebro, and to ask aid from France.

Meanwhile a second disaster followed hard on the heels of the Battle of Baylen. The English Government had sent a small army to Portugal, under Sir Arthur Wellesley, an officer well known for his gallant services in India. This force routed at Vimiero (August 21, 1808) the French troops under Junot, which had occupied Lisbon. The defeat was so crushing that the enemy might have been pursued and driven into the sea without much further trouble. But Wellesley was superseded by a senior officer, Sir Hew Dalrymple, who arrived from England on the night of the battle. This cautious general admitted the French to terms, and by his Convention of Cintra (August 30,

1808), Junot's troops were allowed to quit Portugal with bag and baggage, and to return to France by sea.

Two such checks to the French arms called Bonaparte himself into the field. He hurried over the Pyrenees more than 200,000 of the veterans who had conquered at Austerlitz and Jena and hurled himself upon the Spaniards. The latter were as inferior in numbers as in discipline and military spirit: their ill-organised bands were scattered in all directions, and Napoleon entered Madrid in triumph, and replaced his brother on the throne (December 4, 1808). He hoped to complete the conquest of the Peninsula by crushing the English Army from Portugal, which was now advancing towards him under Sir John Moore—Dalrymple and Wellesley had been recalled to answer before a court-martial for the Convention of Cintra. The emperor moved in his troops from all sides to surround the 25,000 English, but Moore executed an admirably timed retreat, and drew the bulk of the French Army after him into the inhospitable mountains of Galicia.

While vainly pursuing the English, Bonaparte suddenly received news which changed all his plans: a new war was imminent in his rear. Austria had now had three years in which to recover from the humiliation of Austerlitz and had completely reorganised her army. She was chafing bitterly against Napoleon's dictatorial ways and the restraints of the "Continental System." Seeing the French busy in the Spanish war, she gladly listened to the persuasions of the Perceval cabinet, who offered English aid for a fresh attack on the old enemy. It was the news of this danger in the rear which forced Bonaparte to quit Spain, taking with him his imperial guards, but leaving the rest of his troops behind him. Marshal Soult, to whom the pursuit of Moore was handed over, followed the English to the sea: at Corunna the retreating army, suddenly turned to bay, inflicted a sharp defeat on Soult, and embarked in safety for England (January 16, 1809). Moore fell in the moment of victory, after having taught his followers that the French could be outmanoeuvred, outmarched, and beaten in the open field. His troops had suffered much from their own indiscipline and the bitter weather, but little from the overwhelming force of pursuers.

The Austrian war of 1809 was the most formidable struggle in which Bonaparte had yet engaged. The enemy fought better and were far better managed than in 1800 or 1805: they had also the advantage of the fact that 200,000 of the best troops of France were locked up in the Peninsula. The Archduke Charles, Austria's great general, long held Napoleon in check, and even forced him to recross the Danube after the Battle of Essling. It was not until after many months of bitter fighting that the invaders at last gained a decisive battle at Wagram (July 6, 1809). The fortune of war might perhaps have been turned against the French by the help of England; but the Perceval cabinet most unwisely wasted a fine army by sending it into the swamps of Holland to besiege Flushing and make a vain demonstration on Antwerp. Forty thousand men, who might have overrun North Germany, or recovered Madrid, captured Flushing, but suffered so severely from marsh-fever in the pestilential isle of Walcheren that they had at last to be withdrawn, without having aided the Austrians in the least.

Francis II., meanwhile, was forced after Wagram to sign the peace of Schönbrunn, by which he gave up to Napoleon his whole sea-coast in Dalmatia and Illyria, part of Poland, and—bitterest of humiliations—the hand of his daughter Maria Louisa (October 14, 1809). To make this marriage possible, the French emperor callously divorced Josephine Beauharnais, the amiable if frivolous spouse who had shared his fortunes for fourteen years. If he hoped to bind Austria firmly to him by the match, Bonaparte was woefully deceived.

While the Austrian war was being fought out, the French made little progress in Spain. They were now being opposed not only by the Spanish levies, but by a new English Army headed by Wellesley, who had been sent back to the Peninsula when it was recognised that he had been in no wise responsible for the Convention of Cintra. The year 1809 was very glorious to the English arms: Wellesley first drove Marshal Soult out of Portugal, surprising him at Oporto, and forcing him to flee northward with the loss of all his guns and baggage. Then marching into Spain, he joined a Spanish Army under General Cuesta, and defeated at Talavera (July 28, 1809) the French force which covered Madrid. He might even have won back the capital but for the mulish obstinacy of his colleague, and the military incompetence of the Spanish troops, who could not be trusted except behind entrenchments. Talavera was won entirely by the 23,000 English, their allies refusing to advance even when the battle was won. After this heart-breaking experience Wellesley resolved never to cooperate with a Spanish Army again, and to trust entirely to his own troops.

Meanwhile the news of Talavera caused the French troops from all parts of the Peninsula to concentrate against the little English Army, which had to beat a cautious retreat to the Portuguese frontier. No result had been gained from the incursion into Spain, save that the troops had learnt to look with confidence on their leader, who received as his reward for his two victories the title of Wellington, under which he was to be so well known.

After the peace of Schönbrunn had been signed, Bonaparte commenced to pour reinforcements into Spain, and even spoke of going there himself "to drive the British leopard into the sea." Ultimately, however, he sent instead his ablest lieutenant. Marshal Masséna, with 100,000 fresh troops. The arrival of these new legions gave fresh vigour to the invaders: they overran most of Southern and Eastern Spain, and only failed when they were confronted in Portugal by the indomitable; army of Wellington. The year 1810 was for the English commander the most trying period of the whole war. Masséna marched against him in overpowering strength, and all that was in his power was to play a slow and obstinate game of retreat, turning back on occasion, as at the very skilfully fought Battle of Bussaco (September 27), to check the heads of the French columns.

In this way he led the enemy on to the gates of Lisbon, in front of which he had erected a very elaborate system of fortifications, the celebrated "Lines of Torres Vedras," extending in a triple range all across the peninsula on which the Portuguese capital stands. Masséna knew nothing of the lines till his army was brought up by running into the first of them (October, 1810). He found them so strong that he dared not risk an attack on them and halted irresolute in their front. Wellington had expected this and had prepared for the contingency by sweeping the whole countryside bare of provisions and causing the peasantry to retire into Lisbon. Masséna's host starved in front of the lines for five months, vainly hoping for aid from Spain. But Wellington had cut their line of communication with Madrid by throwing numerous bands of Portuguese militia across the mountain roads, and no food and very few fresh troops came to help the invaders. When his army was almost perishing from famine, Masséna was constrained to take it back to Spain, suffering so dreadfully by the way that he only brought back two-thirds of the men whom he had led into Portugal (March, 1811).

The retreat of the French from before the lines of Torres Vedras was the turning-point of the Peninsular War, and in some degree the turning-point of Napoleon's whole career, for Masséna's march to the gates of Lisbon marked the last and furthest point of his advance towards the conquest of Western Europe. After this the French were always to lose ground. The emperor kept an enormous army in the Peninsula, but he could never wholly master it. No single region of Spain would remain quiet unless it was heavily garrisoned; the moment that troops were withdrawn it blazed up again into insurrection. The Spanish levies were very bad troops in the open field, and were beaten with the utmost regularity, even if they had two men to one against the French.

But they never lost heart, in spite of their defeats; as was remarked at the time, "A Spanish Army was easy to beat, but very hard to destroy." It dispersed after a lost battle, but the survivors came together again in a few days, as self-confident and obstinate as ever. The regular troops gave the French far less trouble than the "Guerillas"—half armed peasantry, half robbers, who lurked in the mountains, refrained from attacking large bodies of men, but were always pouncing down to capture convoys, cut off small isolated detachments, and harass the flanks and rear of troops on the march. They so pervaded the country that the transmission of news from one French Army to another was a matter of serious difficulty; a message was never certain to get safely to its destination unless its bearer was protected by a guard of five hundred men.

The French habitually shot every *guerillero* whom they caught, and in return the insurgents murdered every straggler that fell into their hands. The drain on the strength of the army of occupation caused by this lingering and bloody war of retaliation was appalling. It was not for nothing that Bonaparte called the Peninsular War "the running sore" that sapped his strength.

Meanwhile the emperor was apparently at the very zenith of his power during the years 1809-11. His annexations grew more reckless and iniquitous than ever. He appropriated Holland, expelling his own brother Louis Bonaparte, because he showed some regard for Dutch as opposed to French interests, and had ventured to plead against the "Continental System." Soon after, he annexed the whole German coast-line on the North Sea, and even the south-west corner of the Baltic shore. This again was done in the interest of the Continental System; the Hanseatic towns had not shown sufficient enthusiasm in carrying it out, so he absorbed them and cut short several neighbouring principalities. By this last expansion the "French Empire" stretched from Lubeck to Rome, for the pope had already been evicted from the "Eternal City" in 1809.

In addition, Bonaparte personally ruled the kingdom of Italy, and the Illyrian provinces on the Adriatic. The Rhine Confederation, Switzerland, the Grand Duchy of Warsaw, the French Kings of Spain and Naples were his vassals. Prussia was occupied by his garrisons since 1806. Austria, Russia, Denmark, and Sweden were his more or less willing allies. The English had no friends save in the weak kingdoms of Sicily, Sardinia, and Portugal, and among the still weaker Spanish insurgents.

Meanwhile, even in this dark time, England continued to carry out without following the policy that Pitt had left behind him. The conduct of affairs had passed into the hands of second-rate statesmen like Perceval and Lord Liverpool, but no hesitation was shown, though the National Debt continued to rise with appalling rapidity, and though Napoleon seemed more invincible than ever. The war in Spain was giving England a glimpse of success on land, though her armies had still to act upon the defensive, and to yield ground when the enemy came on in overwhelming numbers. Nation and ministers alike considered themselves irrevocably pledged to the war, and comforted themselves with the thought that Napoleon's empire, built upon force and fraud, and maintaining itself by a cruel oppression of the vanquished, must ultimately fall before the simultaneous uprising of all the peoples of Europe.

The year 1811 had seen the French in Spain checked in their endeavours to resume the invasion of Portugal. Masséna's last approach towards its frontier was stopped dead at the Battle of Fuentes D'Oñoro (May 5). Eleven days later, a bloody fight at Albuera turned back Marshal Soult, who had endeavoured to drive off a part of the English Army that lay further to the south, blockading the fortress of Badajoz (May 16). The French could advance no further, while Wellington, on the other hand, was not yet strong enough to be able to contemplate the invasion of Spain. It was expected in the Peninsula that Napoleon himself would soon appear, to finish the task which his lieutenants had proved unable to carry out. But though he recalled Masséna, he neither came on the scene himself, nor sent any appreciable reinforcements to Spain. He already saw a new war impending over him and had turned all his attention to it.

Russia had not been completely crushed in 1807: her armies had been beaten, but only after a gallant struggle, and it was from a sincere desire for peace, and not from mere necessity, that the Czar Alexander had signed the Peace of Tilsit and accepted the Continental System. Five years' experience of that intolerable burden had convinced him that the friendship of Napoleon was dearly bought by accepting it. His realm was losing more by the complete suspension of its foreign trade than it could lose by open war with France. The great landed proprietors, whose timber, hemp, and wheat had once found a ready market in England, and now could not be sold at all, were furious that they should be ruined to please Bonaparte. Urged on by threats of a conspiracy such as had overthrown his father Paul in 1801, Alexander yielded to the pressure of his nobles, and broke with France.

This led to Napoleon's great invasion of Russia in 1812—a grandiose scheme, doomed from the first to failure, because its framer had not taken into consideration the difficulties involved in moving and feeding a host of 600,000 men in a thinly-populated land, destitute of roads and great towns. The Russians retired before the invaders, removing all stores of food, and causing the peasantry to migrate along with the army. Half the horses of Bonaparte's army had perished, and a third of his men had been starved or had deserted before the enemy indulged him with a serious battle. He defeated them at Borodino (September 7) and entered Moscow, but only to find it deserted and empty. A great fire destroyed the city soon after his arrival, and he was driven to order his starving army to retreat on Lithuania to take winter quarters. But the first frosts of November slew off the exhausted soldiery like flies; the Russians harassed the melting host on his way, till it broke up in utter disorganisation, and Bonaparte finally fled to Paris to organise new forces, leaving his lieutenants the task of bringing back the 30,000 miserable survivors of the "Grand Army," who had struggled out from the Russian snows.

In Spain, too, 1812 was a fatal year for the French arms. Wellington, having received more troops from England, and having thoroughly re-organised the Portuguese Army, resolved to make a bold push into Spain. Early in the year he took by storm the two great frontier fortresses of Ciudad Rodrigo (January, 19) and Badajoz (April 6), striking so swiftly that the armies of succour could not come up in time to save them. This rapid success was bought at the cost of many lives, for the assaults had to be delivered before the fire of the defenders had been subdued; but time was all-important, and the result justified the lavish expense of blood.

Having secured the frontier of Portugal, Wellington pressed forward into Spain, and won the first great victory in which he assumed the offensive, at Salamanca (July 22, 1812). By a sudden master-stroke he crushed in the flank of Marshal Marmont, and "routed 40,000 men in forty minutes." This victory led to the recovery of Madrid and the flight of Joseph Bonaparte from his capital. But, evacuating the other provinces of Spain, the French armies massed themselves to check Wellington's further advance, and before their superior numbers the English had to fall back on the Portuguese frontier. All southern Spain, however, had been cleared of the invaders, who now only held the northern half of the Peninsula.

The next year (1813) saw the complete ruin of Napoleon. When the Russians advanced into Germany, the whole nation rose in arms to aid them. Prussia alone, though she had been mutilated and robbed and oppressed with French garrisons, put 200,000 men into the field. The emperor once more appeared at the head of a vast army, bringing up his last reserves, huge drafts from the army of Spain, and hundreds of thousands of conscripts. But his troops were no longer the veterans of Auster-litz, and his enemies fought with a fury of which he had never before had experience. He gained a few successes in the opening weeks of the struggle, but when his own father-in-law, the Austrian emperor, plunged into the struggle, the odds became too heavy, and at the Battle of Leipzig (October 16-18, 1813) he was overwhelmed by numbers, and suffered a crushing defeat, in which more than half his army was slain or captured.

The enemy pursued him energetically, gave him no time to rally, and entered France at his heels. They had at last learnt to turn his own methods of war against him and knew that a beaten foe must not be allowed time to rally. Crossing the Rhine at midwinter, the allies pushed deep into France. Bonaparte, with the wrecks of his army, made a desperate resistance, but had not a shadow of a chance of success. In spite of his skilful manoeu-vring, and of the splendid-endurance of his troops, he was forced nearer and nearer to Paris. At last, while he was engaged with a mere fraction of the allied host, the bulk of it marched past his flank and stormed the lines in front of the French capital (April 4, 1814). On the news of the fall of Paris, Napoleon's own mar-shals refused to persist in the hopeless struggle and compelled their master to lay down his arms and abdicate. In the rage of the moment the emperor swallowed poison, but his constitution was too strong, and he survived to fall into the hands of the victors. They sent him to honourable exile in the Tuscan island of Elba, whose sovereignty was bestowed upon him.

While the Russians, Prussians, and Austrians had entered France from the north-east, another army of invasion had been pouring into the southern departments. Wellington's campaign of 1813 was the most glorious and successful of all his achievements. In early spring he massed his troops on the north-western frontier of Portugal, and marched rapidly up the valley of the Douro. The French armies, scattered in distant cantonments, could not unite in numbers sufficient to give him battle till he had pushed them as far as Vittoria, at the very foot of the Pyrenees. When they did turn to fight, he beat them, intercepted their line of retreat, captured all their guns and baggage—the proceeds of the six years' plunder of Spain—and drove them headlong into France (June 21, 1813).

After having defeated a month later a last endeavour of Marshal Soult to force his way back into the Peninsula (July 27-30, 1813) at the battles of the Pyrenees, Wellington captured the great frontier fortresses of San Sebastian and Pampeluna. He then crossed into France and spent the winter and the early spring of 1814 in forcing Soult back over the rivers and hills of Bearn and Gascony. Just before Napoleon's fall, one division of his army captured Bordeaux, while he himself with the main body evicted Soult from Toulouse, after the last and one of the bloodiest fights of the Peninsular War (April 14). When the news of peace came, he was in full military occupation of eight French departments, and the two largest towns of Southern France.

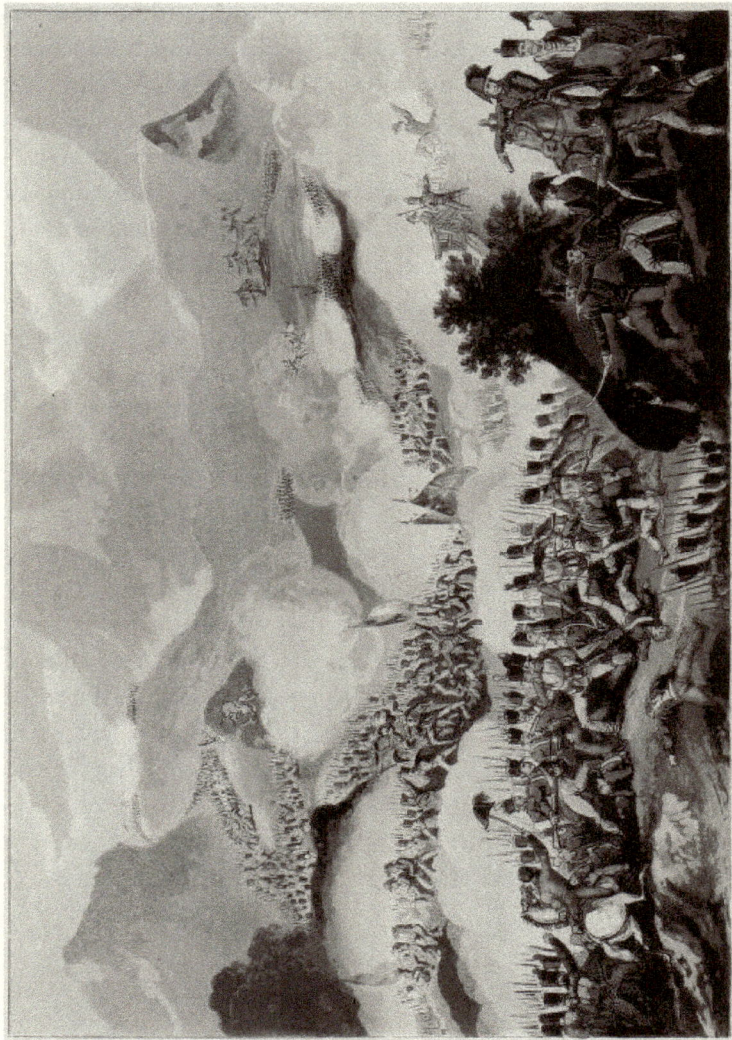

BATTLE OF THE PYRENEES, JULY 25TH, 1813

# CHAPTER 1

# The Nivelle

When the editor of the *United Service Magazine* last did me the honour of publishing some articles of mine on the Peninsular War, we followed the adventures of the British Army from Torres Vedras to the Pyrenees. We passed "the rocks which part Hispania's land from Gaul," and, having described the storming of San Sebastian and the passage of the Bidassoa—both noteworthy incidents, fit to be ranged with any similar incidents of modern European or American warfare—we left the British still besieging Pampeluna on their right. It yielded, having endured all the extremities of famine, on the 31st October, 1813. But the genius of Marshal Soult was above defeat. Adversity suited his temperament and best displayed his capacity.

The month's respite afforded by the prolonged defence of Pampeluna was turned to good account. His strength was augmented by the arrival of 16,000 recruits, and the victorious British Army found itself faced by a tremendous series of fortifications, behind which 70,000 brave Frenchmen awaited the British attack.

While Wellington's army was thus employed inside the southern boundaries of France, he took the utmost precautions to minimise for its trading and agricultural classes the evils of war. Pillage he strictly forbade, and sent home large numbers of Spanish troops who would retaliate on the enemies who had foraged in Andalusia and Castille. But the motives of generals, like those of other men, are very variously interpreted, and what we call the splendid humanity of Wellington in sternly repressing pillage, is ascribed by French writers to the cool duplicity of British policy. The people of the country were enthusiastic in praise of the liberal purchases and of the moderation of their invaders. Had the Spanish system of plunder been allowed to prevail, the result would have been disastrous to the success of the Allies. Had not the rights of person and property been respected, the result would have been a fierce guerilla war. As Lapene says:

> These degenerate Frenchmen, who preferred their market profits to their country's independence, ought to have known that the exemplary discipline of the Anglo-Portuguese was due to the policy rather than to the principles of their leaders. In fact, the difficulties and dangers of invading such a country were matters of the utmost anxiety to their generals. Indeed, history convinced the British Government that an invasion of France was a very risky undertaking, and that Charles V. of Spain himself would have probably failed in an invasion, even after all the losses of 1812-1813, had he crossed the Pyrenees. Had the British general tolerated any licence amidst a population almost driven to despair by the wholesale requisitions and retreat of its own soldiers, what might not have occurred? But as they protected the peasants, these became lethargic, and there was no national rising.

But whatever may have been the motives of Wellington's moderation, its results were satisfactory to all parties except Spanish marauders. I quote Wellington on the bad supply system of the Spaniards.

> More than half of Spain has been cleared of the enemy above a year, and the whole of Spain, excepting Catalonia and a small part of Aragon, since the months of May and June last. The most abundant harvest has been reaped in all parts of the country; millions of money, spent by the contending armies, are circulating everywhere, and yet your armies, however weak in numbers, are literally starving. The allied British and Portuguese Armies under my command have been subsisted, particularly lately, almost

STORMING OF SAN SEBASTIAN AUGUST 31ST, 1813

exclusively upon the magazines imported by sea, and I am concerned to inform your excellency that besides money for pay of all the armies, which has been given from the military chest of the British Army, and has been received from no other quarter, the British magazines have supplied quantities of provisions to all the Spanish armies, in order to enable them to remain in the field at all.

And notwithstanding this assistance, I have had the mortification of seeing the Spanish troops on the outposts obliged to plunder the nut and apple trees for subsistence, and to know that the Spanish troops employed in the blockade were, at the same time, receiving their full allowance. The system, then, is insufficient to procure supplies for the army, and at the same time, I assure your excellency, it is the most oppressive and injurious to the country that could be devised.

It cannot be pretended the country does not produce means of maintaining the men necessary for its defence; those means are undoubtedly superabundant; and the enemy has proved that armies can be maintained in Spain at the expense of the Spanish nation, infinitely larger than are necessary for its defence.

Doubtless Wellington was very cautious and slow, but the celebrated Belgian engineer. General Brialmont, gives an explanation which is of much interest at the present time (1907) to all Britons:

As commander-in-chief, Wellington was obliged to obey politicians who knew nothing about military matters, and yet had the impudence to direct them—a proceeding which turned out to be as ruinous as it was ridiculous, but which was quite in harmony with the spirit of the English Constitution. . . . The commander-in-chief under such a constitution, where nothing can be done without partisan preoccupations, must constantly discuss tactics with the responsible ministers, and furnish them with justificatory documents and information of every kind from which no

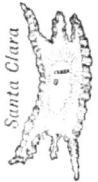

# Attack of
# SAN SEBASTIAN

between 11th July & 9th September
1813.

MONTE OLIA

Passages del Calzuda

Artillery Depot

Right of the Attack

River Urumea

Low water mark

Low water mark

Match of Portuguese Columns

Battery of St. Elmo

Battery Principe

Mirador

MONTE ORGULLO

Hospital

Castle of La Mota

Sta. Catalina (burnt)

Bridge (burnt)

Cask Redoubt

Suburb of St. Martin

Convent & Heights of St. Bartolomeo

Left of the Attack

Convent of Antigua

### Scale of Yards
0  100  200  300                    600

### Santa Clara

### Reference.

1. Convent of Sta. Teresa
2. Arsenal
3. Great Square
4. Flat or Cavalier Bastion
5. Mine sprung by the besiegers
6. Mine sprung by the garrison

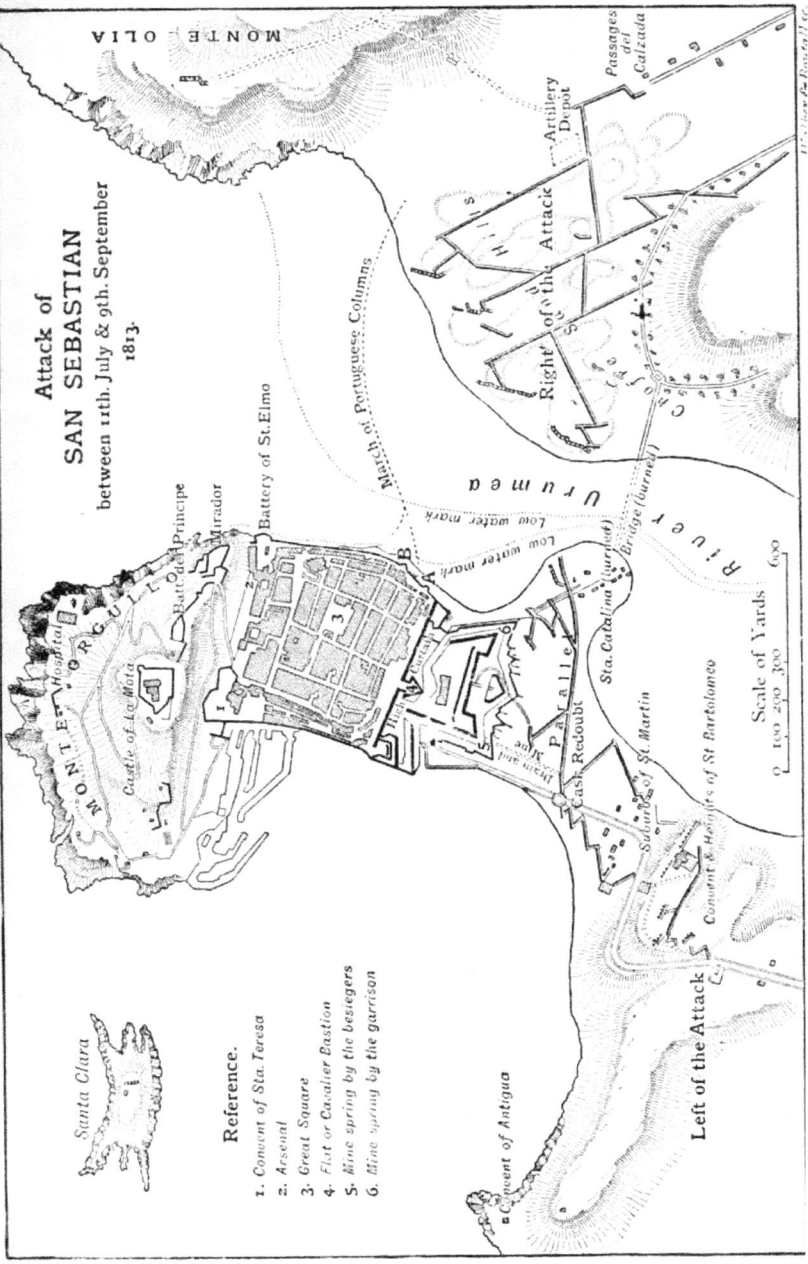

one but the enemy gets any benefit. . . . Everything is discussed—men, horses, money, *matériel*; plans of attack and defence; and when votes of credit are delayed, or the ministers are hampered by the ill will of the majority of the Parliament—behold! the army is left without resources. A general must support his army by temporary expedients . . . a campaign is delayed, hampered, lost!

General Foy, dwelling on the slowness and caution of Wellington, says that it was due partly to the political and administrative conditions under which his army worked, and which were fatal to *initiative*. With this criticism Napier agrees. But both also comment on the slowness of his pursuits, and the lack of striking or risky manoeuvres. On this point Foy quotes the satirical sentences of a very clever brochure, *Advice to the Officers of the British Army*. I give a free translation, which I commend to Bishop Welldon and other fanatical champions of "game-made character."

Nothing can be more laudable than generosity to our enemy. To pursue him rapidly after a victory would be taking a mean advantage of his misfortunes. It suffices to have proved that you can fight him when you think fit. Now, *do play the game*, and act honourably to your adversaries. Be open: don't sneak success by ambuscades; don't head him off; don't attack by night. These things may be war, 'but they are not cricket.'

Think of the honourable fashion in which Hector fought Ajax, when he asked Heaven not to help him, as it would not be fair play. When the enemy is beaten and retires, give him a few days' start—so as to prove that you can beat him again once he is ready. Your generosity will be appreciated, and he will not stop and fight you in an open position. Let him take up a good fortified position, and then attack him again fairly and with deliberation.

But, notwithstanding all this satire against their strategy, Foy, like Müffling, admits that:

Throughout the Peninsular War, as at Waterloo, the British soldier was the soldier of battle. To lead on to the battle-field troops fresh and well-fed, to post them with advantage, and then to await attack with *sang-froid*, behold the perfection of art according to British generals!

I am about to introduce a novelty into this work. I have always held that my readers would much prefer the stirring original narrative of a participator in great events, or the eloquent phrases of a great historian, to any *précis* or rehash of immortal works by a writer like myself; and hence I have always got permission from leading publishers to quote wholesale. For this method I have been heartily, and perhaps fairly, ridiculed. But now I feel on safe ground. This my policy was recommended to officers in the Official Report of the Promotion Examinations, November, 1905. I quote only one sentence:

> For any soldier, Wellington's despatches are profitable and interesting reading, and for the Peninsular Campaign they are naturally most valuable; but, judging from the papers sent in, few candidates had referred to them.

I have always held this opinion: but how are officers to get at these reports? Colonel Gurwood's Selections, published in 1842, are out of print; and the long array of despatches themselves are not available except in great central libraries. I therefore determined, if possible, to include a few despatches in my articles on the new course, and my publishers at once agreed that nothing more instructive and interesting could well be circulated. I therefore applied to Mr. John Murray, whose firm published Colonel Gurwood's book in 1842. By return of post, in the kindest manner, I got permission to use the despatches, and to publish several *in extenso*.

This admirable publisher is full of patriotic zeal to help officers and to illustrate the prowess of his race. Instead, therefore, of wearying my readers with my own words, I can present them with the masterly comments and descriptions of the man who was responsible—a man who regularly worked at the study of military history, all through his career, for four hours a day,

1799-1819; and, moreover, like Napoleon, was a master of his own language.

I now resume my narrative, only in the very words of Wellington.

To Earl Bathurst.

St. Pé, 13th Nov., 1813.

The enemy has, since the beginning of August, occupied a position with their right upon the sea in front of St. Jean de Luz and on the left of the Nivelle, their centre on La Petite Rhune and on the heights behind that village; and their left, consisting of two divisions of infantry under the Comte d'Erlon, on the right of that river, on a strong height in rear of Ainhoue, and on the mountain of Mondarrain, which protected the approach to that village. They had one division under General Foy at St. Jean Pied de Port, which was joined by one of the Army of Aragon, under General Paris, at the time when the left of the Allied Army crossed the Bidassoa.

General Foy's division joined those on the heights behind Ainhoue, when Sir R. Hill moved into the valley of Baztan. The enemy, not satisfied with the natural strength of this position, had the whole of it fortified; and their right in particular had been made so strong that I did not deem it expedient to attack it in front.

Pampeluna having surrendered on the 31st October, and the right of the army having been disengaged from covering the blockade of that place, I moved Lieut.-General Sir R. Hill on the 6th and 7th into the valley of Baztan as soon as the state of the roads, after recent rains, would permit, intending to attack the enemy on the 8th; but the rain which fell on the 7th having again rendered the roads impracticable, I was obliged to defer the attack till the 10th, when we completely succeeded in carrying all the positions on the enemy's flank, left, and centre, in separating the former from the latter; and by these means turning the enemy's strong positions occupied by the right on the lower Nivelle, which they were obliged to evacuate during the night; having taken 51 pieces of cannon and 1,400 prisoners.

The object of the attack being to force the enemy's centre and to establish our army in rear of their right, the attack was made in columns of divisions, each led by the general officer commanding it, and each forming its own reserve. Lieut.-General Sir R. Hill directed the movements of the right, consisting of the 2nd division under Lieut.-General the Hon. Sir W. Stewart, the 6th division under Lieut.-General Sir H. Clinton, a Portuguese division under Lieut.-General Sir J. Hamilton, a Spanish division under General Morillo, Colonel Grant's brigade of cavalry, a brigade of Portuguese artillery under Lieut.-Colonel Tulloh, and three mountain guns under Lieut. Robe, which attacked the position of the enemy behind Ainhoue.

Marshal Sir W. Beresford directed the movements of the right of the centre, consisting of the 3rd division under Major-General the Hon. C. Colville, the 7th division under Marshal de Campo Le Cor, and the 4th division under Lieut.-General the Hon. Sir L. Cole.

The latter attacked the redoubts in front of Sarre, that village, and the heights behind it, supported on their left by the Army of the Reserve of Andalusia, under the command of Marshal de Campo Don P. A. Giron, which attacked the enemy's positions on the right of Sarre on the slopes of La Petite Rhune, and the heights behind the village on the left of the 4th division.

Major-General C. Baron Alten attacked, with the Light Division and General Longa's Spanish division, the enemy's positions on La Petite Rhune, and having carried them, cooperated with the right of the centre in the attack of the heights behind Sarre.

General V. Alten's brigade of cavalry, under the direction of Lieut.-General Sir S. Cotton, followed the movement of the centre; and there were three brigades of British artillery with this part of the army, and three mountain guns with General Giron, and three with Major-General C. Alten.

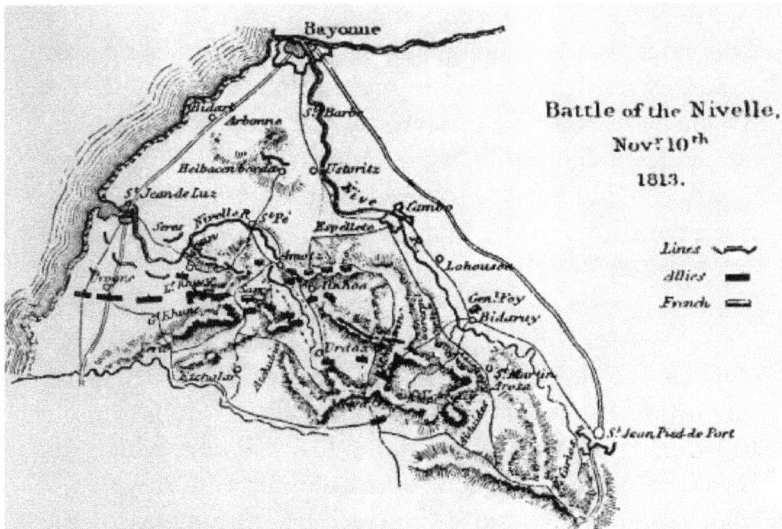

Battle of the Nivelle.
Nov.r 10.th 1813.

Lines
Allies
French

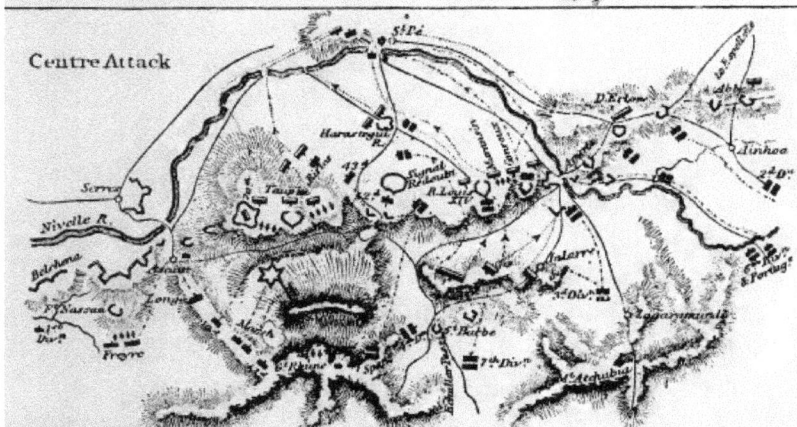

Centre Attack

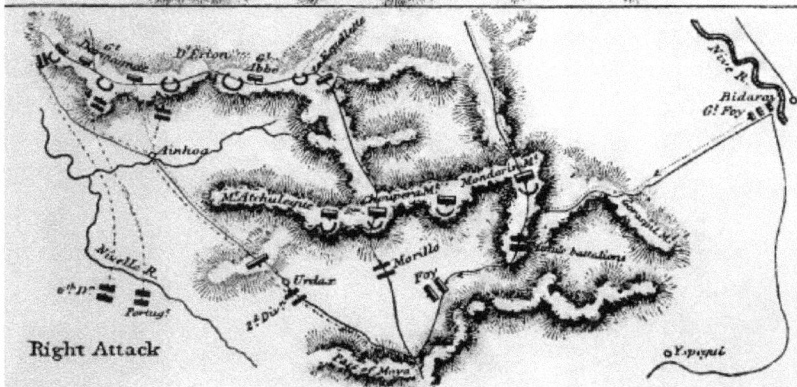

Right Attack

Lieut.-General Don M. Freyre moved in two columns from the heights of Mandale towards Ascain, in order to take advantage of any movement the enemy might make from the right of their position towards their centre; and Lieut.-General Sir J. Hope, with the left of the army drove in the enemy's outposts in front of their entrenchments on the lower Nivelle, carried the redoubt above Urrugne, and established himself on the heights immediately opposite Siboure, in readiness to take advantage of any movement made by the enemy's right.

The attack began at daylight; and Lieut.-General Sir L. Cole having obliged the enemy to evacuate the redoubt on their right in front of Sarre by a cannonade, and that in front of the left of the village having been likewise evacuated on the approach of the 7th division, under General Le Cor, to attack it, Lieut.-General Sir L. Cole attacked and possessed himself of the village, which was turned on its left by the 3rd division under Major-General the Hon. C. Colville; and on its right by the Reserve of Andalusia under Don P. A. Giron; and Major-General C. Baron Alten carried the positions on La Petite Rhune. The whole then co-operated in the attack of the enemy's position behind the village.

The 3rd and 7th divisions immediately carried the redoubts on the left of the enemy's centre, and the Light Division those on the right; while the 4th division, with the Reserve of Andalusia on their left, attacked the positions in their centre. By these attacks the enemy were obliged to abandon their strong positions which they had fortified with much care and labour; and they left in the principal redoubt on the height the 1st battalion 88th Regiment, which immediately surrendered.

While these operations were going on in the centre, I had the pleasure of seeing the 6th division under Lieut.-General Sir H. Clinton, after having crossed the Nivelle, and having driven in the enemy's picquets on both banks, and having covered the passage of the Portuguese division under Lieut.-General Sir J. Hamilton on its right, make a most handsome attack upon the right of the enemy's position behind Ainhoue and on the right of the Nivelle, and carry all the entrenchments and the redoubt on that flank. Lieut.-General Sir J. Hamilton supported, with the Portuguese division, the 6th division on its right; and both co-operated in the attack of the second redoubt, which was immediately carried.

Major-General Pringle's brigade of the 2nd division, under the command of Lieut.-General Sir W. Stewart, drove in the enemy's picquets on the Nivelle and in front of Ainhoue, and Major-General Byng's brigade of the 2nd division carried the entrenchments and a redoubt further on the enemy's left, in which attack the Major-General and these troops distinguished themselves. Major-General Morillo covered the advance of the whole to the heights behind Ainhoue, by attacking the enemy's posts on the slopes of Mondarrain, and following them towards Itassu. The troops on the heights behind Ainhoue were, by these operations under the direction of Lieut.-General Sir R. Hill, forced to retire towards the bridge of Cambo, on the Nive, with the exception of the division on Mondarrain, which, by the march of a part of the 2nd division under Lieut.-General Sir W. Stewart, was pushed into the mountains towards Baygorry.

As soon as the heights were carried on both banks of the Nivelle, I directed the 3rd and 7th divisions, being the right of our centre, to move by the left of that river upon St. Pé, and the 6th division by the right of the river on the same place, while the 4th and Light Divisions and General Giron's Reserve, held the heights above Ascain, and covered this movement on that side, and Lieut.-General Sir R. Hill covered it on the other.

A part of the enemy's troops had retired from their centre, and had crossed the Nivelle at St. Pé; and as soon as the 6th division approached, the 3rd division, under Major-General the Hon. C. Colville, and the 7th division, under

General Le Cor, crossed that river, and attacked and immediately gained possession of the heights beyond it. We were thus established in the rear of the enemy's right; but so much of the day was now spent, that it was impossible to make any further movement, and I was obliged to defer our further operations till the following morning.

The enemy evacuated Ascain in the afternoon, of which village Lieut.-General Don M. Freyre took possession, and quitted all their works and positions in front of St. Jean de Luz during the night, and retired upon Bidart, destroying all the bridges of the lower Nivelle. Lieut.-General Sir J. Hope followed them with the left of the army as soon as he could cross the river; and Marshal Sir W. Beresford moved the centre of the army as far as the state of the road, after a violent fall of rain, would allow, and the enemy retired again on the night of the 11th into an intrenched camp in front of Bayonne.

In the course of the operations, of which I have given Your Lordship an outline, in which we have driven the enemy from positions which they had been fortifying with great labour for three months, in which we have taken 51 pieces of cannon and six tumbrils of ammunition, and 1,400 prisoners, I have great satisfaction in reporting the good conduct of all the officers and troops.

The report itself will show how much reason I had to be satisfied with the conduct of Marshal Sir W. Beresford and of Lieut.-General Sir R. Hill, who directed the centre and right of the army: and with that of Sir L. Cole, Sir W. Stewart, Sir J. Hamilton, and Sir H. Clinton; Major-Generals the Hon. C. Colville and C. Baron Alten; Mariscal de Campo F. Le Cor, and Mariscal de Campo Don P. Morillo, commanding divisions of infantry; and with that of Don P. A. Giron, commanding the Reserve of Andalusia.

Lieut.-General Sir R. Hill, and Marshal Sir. W. Beresford, and these general officers have reported their sense of the conduct of the generals and troops under their command respectively; and I particularly request Your Lordship's attention to the conduct of Major-General Byng, and of Major-General Lambert, who conducted the attack of the 6th division. I likewise particularly observed the gallant conduct of the 51st and 68th regiments, under the command of Major Rice and Lieut.-Colonel Hawkins, in Major-General Inglis' brigade, in the attack of the heights above St. Pé, in the afternoon of the 30th. The 8th Portuguese brigade, in the 3rd division under Major-General Power, likewise distinguished themselves in the attack of the left of the enemy's centre; and Major-General Anson's brigade of the 4th division, in the village of Sarre and the centre of the heights.

Although the most brilliant part of this service did not fall to the lot of Lieut.-General Sir J. Hope and Lieut.-General Don M. Freyre, I had every reason to be satisfied with the mode in which these general officers conducted the service of which they had the direction.

Our loss, although severe, has not been so great as might have been expected, considering the strength of the positions attacked, and the length of time, from daylight in the morning till night, during which the troops were engaged; but I am concerned to add that Colonel Barnard of the 95th has been severely, though I hope not dangerously, wounded; and that we have lost in Lieut.-Colonel Lloyd of the 94th an officer who had frequently distinguished himself, and was of great promise.

I received the greatest assistance in forming the plan for this attack, and throughout the operations, from the Quartermaster-General Sir G. Murray, and the Adjutant-General the Hon. Sir E. Pakenham; and from Lieut.-Colonels Lord Fitzroy Somerset and Campbell, and all the officers of my personal staff, and H.S.H. the Prince of Orange.

The artillery, which was in the field, was of great use to us; and I cannot sufficiently acknowledge the intelligence and activity with which it was brought to the point of attack under the direction of Colonel Dickson, over the bad roads through the mountains in this season of the year.

CHAPTER 2

# Bayonne

Our last chapter dealt with the storming of the French works on the Nivelle—an operation which must rank with the most brilliant enterprises of Lee or Grant, or with the fierce resolution of the Japanese at the Scha Ho and the Hun Ho. But though the distance from the redoubts, so ably carried and so splendidly defended on the 10th November, to Bayonne was only a good day's march, the natural obstacles were of enormous difficulty. The other difficulties of the British general from the conduct of his allies, and the scarcity of supplies, and the lack of efficient co-operation of the navy, and the folly of our politicians, were still more trying. Hence it was not till the 13th December that our army was master of both banks of the Nive, and not till February that Soult left the fortress of Bayonne to its own resources, and abandoned the entrenched camp which had been so long his pivot of operations.

It will be observed that when Soult held the bridges of Bayonne, and the British tried to close in on him on both banks of the river, he was in a position of interior lines very nearly the same as that occupied by Jackson in the Shenandoah Valley, 1862, as against Shields and Fremont, and similar to that which Lee occupied in the same year on the Chickahominy as against Porter and MacClellan, and not unlike that which the Archduke Charles occupied, in 1796, on the Danube, at Ingoldstadt as against Jourdan and Moreau, and that which Napoleon occupied, in 1814, at Nogent, against Blücher and Schwartzenberg.

He was in possession of the bridges, and hence, once the enemy divided and was astride the river he could throw his centre to the help of his wings on either side of the river alternately, and thus defeat each portion of the divided enemy in turn.

It is true that the Nive was a transverse obstacle to the advance of the British as they looked north, but, once they made a wheel to their left from the Nivelle towards Bayonne, it became a parallel obstacle, and hence very difficult from a strategic point of view, and the scene of most instructive and very able tactics as well as strategy on both sides—not a point of vantage or ruse of advantage was ignored by either army, whose leaders had now become past masters of their art.

After sending all the Spanish, 25,000 men, out of France except Morillo's force, which had abstained from pillage, Wellington had 80,000 men, including 8,600 horse and 100 guns.

In pursuance of our plan, I now quote Wellington's despatch on the Battle of the Nive.

To Earl Bathurst.

St. Jean de Luz, 14th Dec, 1813.

Since the enemy's retreat from the Nivelle they had occupied a position in front of Bayonne, which had been entrenched with great labour since the battle fought at Vittoria in June last. It appears to be under the fire of the works of the place; the right rests upon the Adour, and the front in this part is covered by a morass occasioned by a rivulet which falls into the Adour.

The right of the centre rests upon this same morass, and its left upon the River Nive; the left is between the Nive and the Adour, on which river the left rests. They had their advance posts from their right in front of Angelet and towards Biarritz. With their left they defended the river Nive, and communicated with General Paris's division of the Army of Catalonia, which was at St. Jean Pied de Port; and they had a considerable corps cantoned in Ville Franque and Mougerre.

It was impossible to attack the enemy in this position as long as they remained in force in it without the certainty of a great loss; at the same time, that success was not very

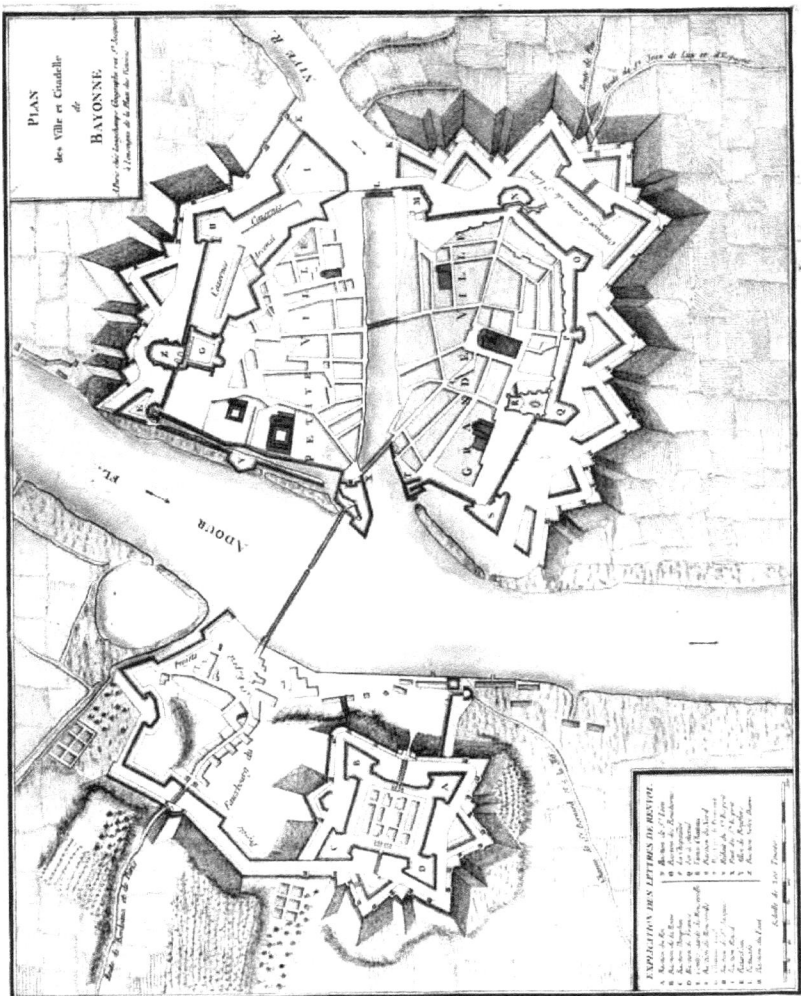

PLAN
des Ville et Citadelle
de
BAYONNE

ADOUR

ADOUR

EXPLICATION DES LETTRES DE BAYONNE.

probable, as the camp is so immediately protected by the works of the place. It appeared to me, therefore, that the best mode of obliging the enemy either to abandon the position altogether or at least so to weaken his force in it as to offer the more favourable opportunity of attacking it, was to pass the Nive, and to place our right upon the Adour; by which operation the enemy, already distressed for provisions, would lose the means of communication with the interior afforded by that river, and would become still more dispersed.

The passage of the Nive was likewise calculated to give us other advantages: to open to us a communication with the interior of France for intelligence, etc., and to enable us to draw some supplies from the country.

I had determined to pass the Nive immediately after the passage of the Nivelle, but was prevented by the bad state of the roads, and the swelling of all the rivulets occasioned by the fall of rain in the beginning of that month; but the state of the weather and roads having at length enabled me to collect the materials, and make the preparations for forming bridges for the passage of that river, I moved the troops out of their cantonments on the 8th, and ordered that the right of the army, under Lieut.-General Sir R. Hill, should pass on the 9th and in the neighbourhood of Camo, while Marshal Sir W. Beresford should favour and support his operation by passing the 6th division, under Lieut.-General Sir H. Clinton, at Ustaritz.

Both operations succeeded completely. The enemy were immediately driven from the right bank of the river, and retired towards Bayonne by the great road, from the right bank of the river, of St. Jean Pied de Port. Those posted opposite Cambo were nearly intercepted by the 6th division, and one regiment was driven from the road and obliged to march across the country.

The enemy assembled in considerable force on a range of heights running parallel with the Adour, and still keeping Villa Franque by the right. The 8th Portuguese Regiment under Colonel Douglas, and the 9th Caçadores under Colonel Brown, and the British light infantry battalion of the 6th division, carried this village and the heights in the neighbourhood. The rain which had fallen the preceding night, and on the morning of the 8th, had so destroyed the road that the day had nearly elapsed before Sir R. Hill's corps had come up, and I was, therefore, satisfied with the possession of the ground which we occupied.

On the same day Lieut.-General Sir J. Hope, with the left of the army under his command, moved forward by the great road from St. Jean de Luz towards Bayonne, and reconnoitred the right of the entrenched camp under Bayonne, and the course of the Adour below the town, after driving in the enemy's post from the neighbourhood of Biarritz and Angelet. The Light Division, under Major-General von Alten, likewise moved forward from Bassasarry and reconnoitred that part of the enemy's entrenchments.

Sir J. Hope and Major-General Alten retired immediately to the ground they had before occupied.

On the morning of the 10th, Lieut.-General Sir R. Hill found that the enemy had retired from the position which they had occupied the day before on the heights, into the entrenched camp on that side of the Nive; and he, therefore, occupied the position intended for him, with his right towards the Adour and his left at Ville Franque, and communicating with the centre of the army, under Marshal Sir W. Beresford, by a bridge laid over the Nive, and the troops under the marshal were again drawn to the left of the Nive.

General Morillo's division of Spanish infantry, which had remained with Sir R. Hill when the other Spanish troops went into cantonment within the Spanish country, was placed at Urcuray, with Colonel Vivian's brigade of light dragoons at Hasparren, in order to observe the movements of the enemy's division under General Paris, which, upon our passage of the Nive, had retired towards St. Palasi

41

BATTLE OF THE BIDASSOA OCTOBER 7TH, 1813

On the 10th, in the morning, the enemy moved out of the entrenched camp with their whole army, with the exception of what occupied the works opposite Sir R. Hill's position, and drove in the picquets of the Light Division and of Sir J. Hope's corps, and made a most desperate attack upon him, the post of the former at the *château* and Church of Arcangues, and upon the advanced posts of the latter on the high road from Bayonne to St. Jean de Luz, near the mayor's house at Biarritz.

Both attacks were repulsed in the gallant style by the troops, and Sir J. Hope's corps took about 500 prisoners. The brunt of the action with Sir J. Hope's advance posts fell upon the first Portuguese Brigade under Major-General Archibald Campbell, which were on duty, and upon Major-General Robinson's brigade of the 5th division, which moved up to their support.

Lieut.-General Sir J. Hope reports most favourably of the conduct of these, and of all the other troops engaged; and I had great satisfaction in finding that this attempt made by the enemy upon our left, in order to oblige us to draw in our right, was completely defeated by a comparatively small part of our force.

I cannot sufficiently applaud the ability, coolness, and judgment of Sir J. Hope, who, with the general and staff officers under his command, showed the troops an example of gallantry which must have tended to produce the favourable result of the day. Sir J. Hope received a severe contusion, which, however, I am happy to say, has deprived me only for a moment of the benefit of his assistance.

After the action was over the regiments of Nassau and Francfort, under command of Colonel Kruse, came over to the post of Major-General Ross's brigade of the 4th division, which was formed for the support of the centre. When the night closed the enemy was still in large force in front of our posts, on the ground from which they had driven the picquets. They retired, however, during the night from Sir J. Hope's front, leaving posts, which were

BATTLE OF NIVELLE NOVEMBER 10TH, 1813

immediately driven in. They still occupied in force the bridge on which the picquets of the Light Division had stood, and it was obvious that the whole army was still in front of our left; and about three in the afternoon they again drove in Sir J. Hope's picquets and attacked his posts. They were again repulsed with considerable loss.

The attack was recommenced on the morning of the 12th with the same want of success. The 1st division under Major-General Howard having relieved the 5th division, the enemy discontinued it in the afternoon, and retired entirely within the entrenched camp on that night. They never renewed the attack on the posts of the Light Division after the 10th.

Lieut.-General Sir J. Hope reports most favourably of the conduct of all the officers and troops, particularly of the Portuguese brigade under General Archibald Campbell, and of General Robinson's and General Hay's brigade of the 5th division, under the command of Colonel the Hon. C. Greville. He mentions particularly Major-General Hay, commanding the 5th division, Major-Generals Robinson and Bradford, Brigadier-General Campbell, Colonels De Rego and Greville, commanding the 7th brigade; Lieut.-Colonel Lloyd of the 84th, who was unfortunately killed; Lieut.-Colonel Barns of the Royals, and Cameron of the 9th, Captain Ramsay of the R.H.A.; Colonel de Lancey, the deputy quartermaster-general; Lieut.-Colonel Macdonald, the assistant adjutant-general, attached to Sir J. Hope's corps; and the officers of his personal staff.

The 1st division, under Major-General Howard, were not engaged till the 12th, when the enemy's attack was more feeble; but the Guards conducted themselves with their usual spirit.

The enemy, having thus failed in all their attacks with their whole force upon their left, withdrew into their entrenchments on the night of the 12th, and passed a large force through Bayonne, with which, on the morning of the 13th, they made a most desperate attack upon Lieut.-

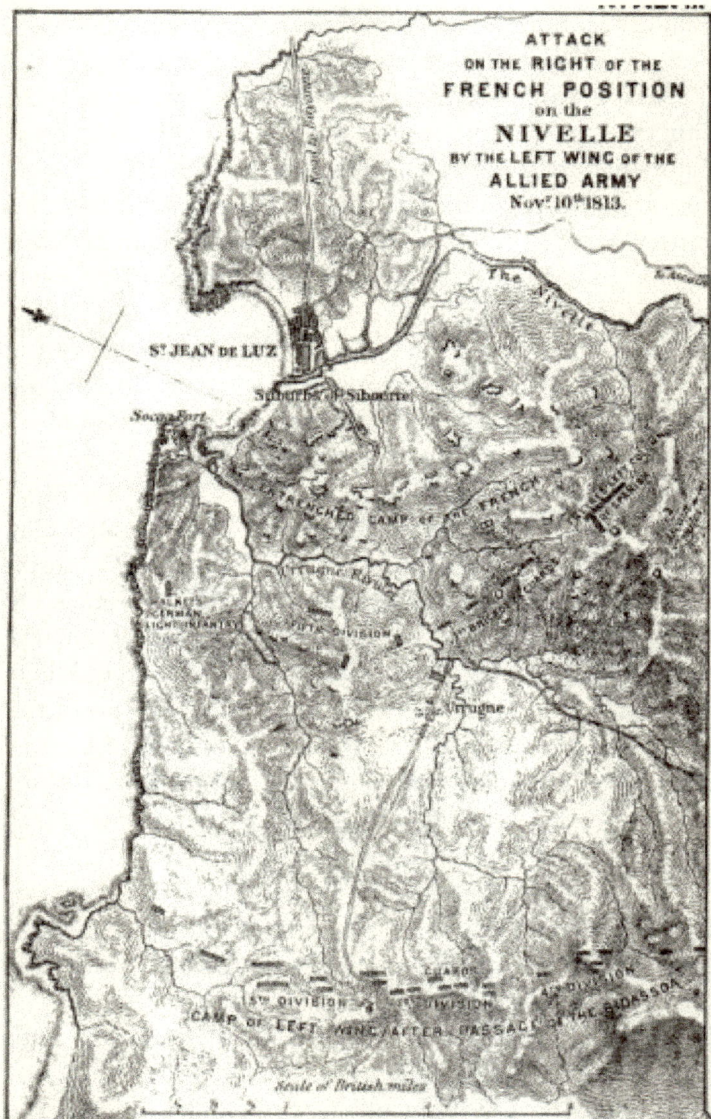

ATTACK
ON THE RIGHT OF THE
FRENCH POSITION
on the
NIVELLE
BY THE LEFT WING OF THE
ALLIED ARMY
Novr 10th 1813.

St JEAN DE LUZ

Suburbs of Siboerre

Socoa Fort

The Nivelle

ENTRENCHED CAMP OF THE FRENCH

1st or K.G.L.
GERMAN
LIGHT INFANTRY

FIFTH DIVISION

Urrugne

1st DIVISION

CAMP OF LEFT WING AFTER PASSAGE OF THE BIDASSOA

Scale of British miles

General Sir R. Hill.

In expectation of this attack I had requested Marshal Sir W. Beresford to reinforce the lieut.-general with the 6th division, which crossed the Nive at daylight in the morning, and I further reinforced him by the 4th division and two brigades of the 3rd division.

The expected arrival of the 6th division gave the Lieut.-General great facility in making his movements; but the troops under his own immediate command had defeated and repulsed the enemy with immense loss before their arrival. The principal attack having been made along the high-road from Bayonne to St, Jean Pied de Port, Major-General Barnes' brigade of British infantry and the 5th brigade of Portuguese infantry, under Brigadier-General Ashworth, were particularly engaged in the contest with the enemy on that point; and these troops conducted themselves admirably.

The Portuguese division of infantry, under the command of Mariscal de Campo F. Le Cor, moved to their support on their left in a very gallant style, and regained an important position between those troops and Major-General Pringle's brigade engaged with the enemy in front of Ville Franque. I have great satisfaction also in observing the conduct of Major-General Byng's brigade of British infantry, supported by the Portuguese brigade under command of Major-General Buchan, in carrying an important height from the enemy on the right of our position, and maintaining it against all their efforts to regain it

Two guns and some prisoners were taken from the enemy, who, being beat in all points and having suffered a terrible loss, were obliged to retire upon their entrenchments.

It gives me the greatest satisfaction to have another opportunity of reporting my sense of the services and merits of Lieut.-General Sir R. Hill upon this occasion, as well as of those of Lieut.-General the Hon. Sir W. Stewart, commanding the 2nd division of the infantry, Major-Generals Barnes, Byng, Pringle, Mariscal de Campo F. Le Cor, Ma-

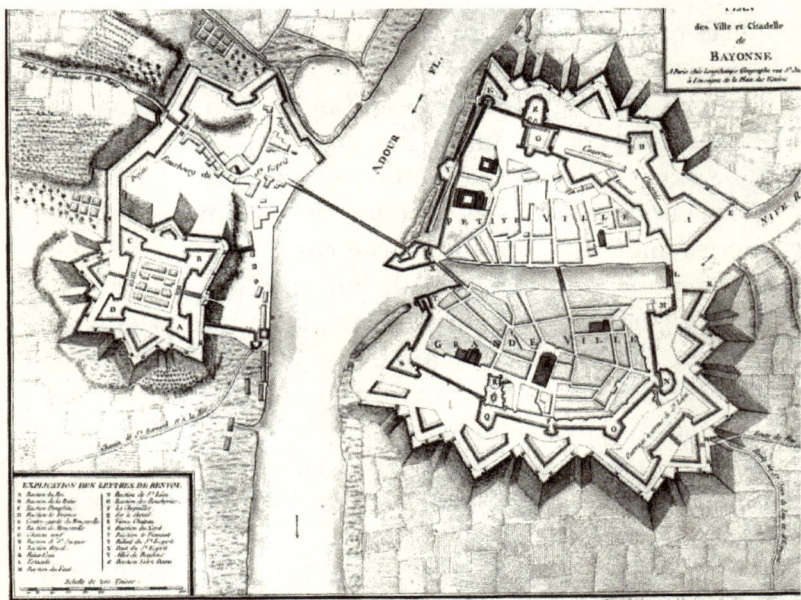

PLAN
des Ville et Citadelle
de
BAYONNE

jor-General Buchan and Da Costa, and Brigadier-General Ashworth. The British artillery under Lieut.-Colonel Ross, and a Portuguese artillery under Colonel Tullch distinguished themselves; and Lieut.-General Sir R. Hill reports particularly the assistance he received from Lieut.-Colonels Bouverie and Jackson, the Assistant Adjutant-General, and Assistant Quartermaster-General attached to his corps, Lieut.-Colonel Goldfinch of the Royal Engineers, and from the officers of his personal staff.

The enemy marched a large body of cavalry across the bridge of the Adour yesterday evening, and retired their force.

Some of General Foy's remarks published by the Comtesse Foy in 1827 are well worth quoting; indeed might well be paraphrases of some recent political speeches. (*Guerre de la Peninsula*, vol. 1.)

The profession of soldier does not attract the British citizen. Hence the army costs an enormous sum to support, equip, and move. If by reason of the insufficiency of recruits the British had recourse to obligatory service to repair losses, the soldiers would soon demand a liberal discipline, Civil Rights, and the army would no longer be the tool of political parties.

Its detachments are scattered all over the globe. Wherever a rock shows its head above the Mediterranean or the Indian Ocean, England has located a few squads of soldiers. It has doubled its army for the progressive invasion and conquest of India; after such a scattering what remains for great military expeditions? Although the British had 500,000 men under arms, they could not send more than 50,000 men to the Peninsula. Hence the most numerous army that the British would send to the Continent would be 50,000 men, and then they would not burn their ships.

The same general idea was set forth by Wellington in deprecating the division of force proposed by the Ministry, as is evident from his despatch to Earl Bathurst. from St. Jean de Luz,

BATTLE OF ST. JEAN DE LUZ DECEMBER 10TH, 1813

21st December, 1813:—

. . . It is the business of the government, and not my business, to dispose of the resources of the nation; and I have no right to give an opinion on the subject. I wish, however, to impress upon Your Lordship's mind that you cannot maintain military operations in the Peninsula and in Holland with British troops; you must either give up the one or the other, as, if I am not mistaken, the British establishment is not equal to the maintenance of two armies in the field.

I began last campaign with 70,000 British and Portuguese troops; and taking away from me the German troops, and adding to me what could be got from the militia, and by enabling me to bring up Portuguese recruits, I expected this year to take the field with 80,000 men; but this is now quite out of the question. If you should form the Hanoverian Army, which is, in my opinion, the most reasonable plan to go upon, I shall not take the field with much more than 50,000 men, unless I shall receive real and efficient assistance to bring up the Portuguese recruits, and it will then be about 55,000, or if our wounded recover well and we have no more actions, about 60,000 men.

Then I beg you to observe that, whenever you extend your assistance to any country, unless at the same time fresh means are put in action, the service is necessarily stinted in all its branches on the old stage. I do not wish to make complaints, but if you will look at every branch of the service here now you will find it stinted, particularly the naval branch and those supplies which necessarily come from England.

I lately sent you a return of the supply of clothing sent for the Spanish Army for the year 1813, from which you will see how that branch stands; and I have not heard of the arrival at Plymouth of the 25,000 suits to be lodged in store there, which will leave a deficiency of 3,000 suits for 1813, 7,800 suits having lately arrived at Coruna. Nearly all the great coats are deficient. The reason of this is that

ATTACK ON THE ROAD TO BAYONNE DECEMBER 13TH, 1813

the interior departments do not observe that when British exertion is to be made on a new scene, the old means are not sufficient. New engines must be set at work; otherwise the service must be stinted in one or both scenes, and there must be complaints.

The different reports which I have sent Your Lordship will show how we stand for want of naval means; and I beg you to take the state and condition of the ships on the stations, striking out those coming and going home, which the Admiralty will insert on the 1st and 15th of every month since June last, and you will see whether or not there is reason to complain. But whatever may be the numbers employed, I complain that there are not enough, because they do not perform the service. This is certainly not the intention of the Admiralty. . . .

Your lordship is also acquainted with the state of our financial resources. We are overwhelmed with debts, and I can scarcely stir out of my house on account of the public creditors waiting to demand payment of what is due to them. Some of the muleteers are twenty-six months in arrears; and only yesterday I was obliged to give them bills upon the Treasury for a part of their demands or lose their services; which bills they will, I know, sell at a depreciated rate of exchange to the sharks who are waiting at Passages, and in this town, to take advantage of the public distresses. I have reason to believe that they became thus clamorous at the instigation of British merchants.

I draw Your Lordship's attention to these facts just to show that Great Britain cannot extend her operations by British troops, or even her pecuniary or other assistance, without starving the service here, unless additional means and exertion should be used to procure what is wanted.

From these profound political and strategic discussions, we turn with pleasure to illustrate the comity of nations, even in the case of armed men, in the deadly struggle of daily conflict. When outposts were placed civility prevailed among the sentries, who were careful not to disturb their own rest and the

**SKETCH**
illustrative of operations
**OF LEFT WING OF ALLIED ARMY**
on the Nive in vicinity of Bayonne
December 1813
and passage of the Adour Feb.ᵏ 14

AA Entrenchments thrown up by British to protect the left of the Army
Scale of English Miles
Miles

plans of their superior officers by unnecessary and desultory and precipitate skirmishes.

About the same time one of Hill's posts near the confluence of the Arun with the Adour was surprised by some French, who remained until fresh troops forced them to repass the river again. This was in retaliation for the surprise of a French post a few days before by the 6th division, which was attended with circumstances repugnant to the friendly habits long established between the French and British troops at the outposts. The value of such a generous intercourse old soldiers well understand, and some illustrations of it at this period may be quoted.

On the 9th December, the 43rd was assembled on an open space within twenty yards of the enemy's out-sentry; yet the latter continued to walk his beat for an hour, relying so confidently on the customary system that he placed his knapsack on the ground to ease his shoulders. When the order to advance was given, one of the soldiers having told him to go away helped him to replace his pack, and the firing then commenced. Next morning the French in like manner warned a 43rd sentry to retire.

A more remarkable instance happened, however, when Wellington, desirous of getting to the top of a hill occupied by the enemy near Bayonne, ordered some riflemen to drive the French away; seeing them stealing up too close as he thought, he called out to fire; but with a loud voice one of those old soldiers replied "no firing!" and holding up the butt of his rifle, tapped it in a peculiar manner.

At the well-understood signal, which meant "we must have the hill for a short time," the French, who, though they could not maintain it, would not relinquish the post without a fight if they had been fired upon, quietly retired. And this signal would never have been made if the post had been one capable of a permanent defence, "so well," as Napier says, "do veterans understand war and its proprieties."

# CHAPTER 3

# Passage of the Adour

Rockets were used for the first time in war by the British, at Leipsic, on the 18th October, 1813. Their effect at the passage of the Adour, 22nd February, 1814, was very considerable. The French flotilla was as much surprised apparently as were the Chitral troops by the use of star shells at the Swat River.

In the night, General Hope cautiously moved the 1st division, the rocket brigade, and six heavy guns, to the sandhills near the mouth of the river; and at daybreak on the following morning, although the stormy contrary winds and violent surf on the coast prevented the arrival of the gunboats and luggers which were intended to have co-operated in the passage, he gallantly resolved to attempt the forcing of the passage alone.

But no sooner were the scarlet uniforms seen emerging from the shelter of the sandhills than their flotilla, which, from the British gunboats not having got up, had the undisputed command of the river, opened a tremendous fire upon them. The British heavy guns and the rocket brigade, which was used for the first time in the Peninsular War, replied with so quick a discharge that part of the flotilla was sunk, and the remainder, in consternation at the awful rush and aspect of the rockets, drew off out of reach of the fire, further up the river.

Upon this, sixty of the Guards were rowed across in a pontoon in face of a French detachment, which was so terrified by the rockets whizzing through their ranks, that they also took to flight. A raft was then formed with the remainder of the pontoons, and a hawser having been stretched across, six hundred of the Guards and the 66th Regiment, with part of the rocket brigade, were passed over. They were attacked by Macomble's French brigade, but it fled in abject terror at the first discharge of the rockets!

Thus, in the advance on Chitral:

A determined rush of the enemy was planned and on the eve of being executed, when the unexpected, and, as it seemed to the enemy, magical appearance of a star shell completely dumfounded the hitherto dauntless foe, and the attack was not delivered. (See *The Relief of Chitral*,' Younghusband.)

### Inaction after the Battle of the Nive.

The reason for the inaction of Lord Wellington from the Battle of the Nive, 10th December, till the skirmish of Hélette against Harispe have been much discussed. Some say that it was because he wished to regulate his movements in conformity with those of the Allies in the valley of the Seine; but this correlation would scarcely compensate for the annoyance, privations of every kind, and losses suffered by the allied army in the early part of 1814.

Moreover, there was a manifest desire on the part of the British Government to transfer Wellington's army by sea to Holland, thus to cooperate with the northern and central European Powers. But Wellington pointed out that the result would be to reinforce Napoleon on the Seine or Rhine by 100,000 good troops, who might turn the tables against the Germans, Russians, and Austrians in Champagne. Indeed, the two divisions of Laval and Boyer were a most valuable reinforcement to Napoleon near Paris.

But Wellington's forces were very cautious; they had to move parallel to the Pyrenees against a strong line, with Bayonne fortress on its right, on the Upper Aire, and over the Gaves with which the country is intersected; and they were loath to assume the offensive against a general like Soult till they were reinforced themselves by 5,000 men, including 1,200 cavalry. Moreover, the whole cavalry of the English Army, which from want of for-

Sketch Map of the
Country round Bayonne.
showing the Passage of the Adour,
& the events of December & February 1813-14.

*Allies* ☐ *French*

N

Gave d'Oleron

To Orthez

Cassanede

To Navarrens

To Sauveterre

Peyrehorade

Port de Lanne

R. Adour

Gave de Pau

Sorde

Hastingues

Overgave

Guiche

R. Bidouze

Bidouze

Bellocq

Came

Sindos

Hauterive

Bastide
de Bearn

Bergoney

Ulherre

Orsanco

Masparraut

Sombérante

Heights of a Montagu

Garris

BATTLE OF
FEB. 15TH. 1814

To St. Palais

St. Palais

St. Martin

Necharp

Isturitz

To St. Jean Pied de Port

St. Esteben

Bonloc

St. Martin

Arberoue

R. Arran

Urt

R. Ardanavi

Briscous

Lahonce

Urcuray

Hasparren

Mendionde

St. Jean P. de Port

Macaye

Mt. Ursuia

R. Nive

To St. Jean de la Port

Lahoussoa

R. Joyeuse

R. Esteben

Urt

R. Adour

River Adour

St. Etienne

Mousserolles

St. Pierre
DEC. 13TH. 1813.

Chateau

Villefranque

Larressore

Bridge of Boats

Villefranque

R. Nive

Arcangues

BATTLE OF
Arbonne OF DEC.10-13. 1813.

Biarritz

Bidart

Anglet

Marrac

Bayonne

Wellington's
Bridge

Bar

PASSAGE OF THE
ADOUR FEB. 23RD. &
24TH. 1814.

Ustaritz

Arauntz

Ustaritz

Halsou

Bas Cambo
Bridge

Cambo

Itxassou

Espelette

St. Pée

Mt. Rhune

PASSAGE OF THE
NIVELLE NOV. 10TH. 1813.

R. Nivelle

To St. Jean de Luz

Walker & Boutall sc.

age during the lull had been sent back to the valley of the Ebro, was now, with the return of spring, brought back to the valley of the Adour.

Nor was Marshal Soult idle in the interval. He instructed his conscripts diligently in the military art. This he did safely under the shelter of Bayonne. But his effective troops were reduced, after deducting the garrison of Bayonne and other forts which he was obliged to defend, to 40,000 men; but of these a considerable part were new troops, disciplined, but not inured to war.

On the other hand, the Anglo-Portuguese state, on the 13th February, 1814, was 60,000 infantry, 10,000 cavalry, and there were also 30,000 Spaniards and 140 guns. As Alison says:

> Considering the discipline and spirit of the greater part of the troops, and the talents and experience of their Chief, it was the most formidable army which had ever been put forth by the power of England.

### Lapene's Reverie by the Banks of the Gave.

Any of my readers who have slept in camps amidst a multitude of armed men will sympathise with the meditations of Lapene in his bivouac by the banks of the Gave, near Orthez. French writers on war have a grand style, and elevate their readers.

> Those whom nature has gifted with the faculty of meditating and thinking strongly—inexhaustible source of great joys as well as of deplorable errors—profit by the calm of the night and the silence of the bivouacs to collect their ideas and to review the memories of the past. Shunning sleep, and in the midst of their sleeping companions, when the watch-fires about to die out only give a feeble and fickle light, their imagination walks abroad amidst their surroundings. It even crosses the limits of the camp, and dwells upon the spectacle offered by the hostile army on the other side of the river.
> Behold, there was the army which less than two years before was also in front of us at the mouth of the Tagus, the Guadiana, and the Guadalquivir, and whose standards re-

tired before ours to Cadiz, to shelter from the fire of our batteries planted on the coasts of Andalusia!

Fifteen months before, these troops had retired before us behind the Tormes into the impracticable roads which traverse the neighbourhoods of Ciudad Rodrigo and the frontiers of Portugal. Is not the French Army, which is today, (1907), halted by the banks of the Gave, the same army whose battalions bivouacked on the banks of the Adige, the Danube, the Vistula, the Niemen?

Have not many amongst us appeared as victors on the banks of the Nile and the Jordan? What great deeds! What riches of memory! What men filled those immortal phalanxes! What a series of reverses! Triumphs exhausted in Europe, the French Army then went to conquer lands beyond the sea, and to realise the ideal expeditions of antiquity. Placed today behind a torrent in the heart of France itself, our ambition only hopes to defend a few leagues of its sacred soil.

Here, indeed, the brilliant Frenchman gives a lesson on the vanity of human wishes. Within a very few years, if we British trifle with our military resources and the skill of our arms, many a British officer by the banks of the Indus, the Nile, the St. Lawrence, the Murray, the Orange, the Shannon, and the Severn will be kept awake by very similar reveries. Let us for eight years more indulge in such political and administrative pasquinades as have befooled us for the past ten years, and Soult's army of 1814 will be avenged in 1914.

The passage of the Bidassoa, the Nivelle, the Nive, the Adour, and the Gave de Pau afford a series of lessons in the skilful use of obstacles, and in the determined and able dislodgments of adversaries from very strong positions, splendidly, fortified and with rivers in front, a series of intersecting positions with few parallels in history. Better illustrations, cannot be found either in Virginian or in Manchurian records,

We now come to the events preceding the Battle of Orthez, and the leading details of that battle, and hence we use. Wellington's despatch 881, dated St. Sever, 1st March, 1814.

To Earl Bathurst.

St. Sever, 1st March, 1814.

The sense which I had of the difficulties attending the. movement of the army by its right, across so many rivers as must have been and as have lately been passed in its progress, induced me to determine to pass the Adour below the town of Bayonne, notwithstanding the difficulties which opposed this operation; and I was the more induced to adopt this plan, as, whatever might be the mode in which I should eventually move upon the enemy, it was obvious that I could depend upon no communication with Spain and the seaports of that kingdom, and with St. Jean de Luz, excepting that alone, which is practicable in the winter, *viz.* by the high-roads leading to and from Bayonne. I likewise hoped that the establishment of a bridge below Bayonne would give me the use of the Adour as a harbour.

The movements of the right of the army, which I detailed to Your Lordship in my last despatch, were intended to divert the enemy's attention from the preparations at St. Jean de. Luz and Pasages for the passage of the Adour below Bayonne, and to induce the enemy to move his force to his left, in which objects they succeeded completely; but upon my return to St. Jean de Luz, on the 19th, I found the weather so unfavourable at sea, and so uncertain, that I determined to push forward my operations on the right, notwithstanding that I had still the Gave d'Oleron, the Gave de Pau, and the Adour to pass.

Accordingly, I returned to Garris on the 21st, and ordered the 6th and light divisions to break from the blockade of Bayonne; and General Don M. Freyre to close up the cantonments of his corps towards Irun, and to be prepared to cross-move when the left of the army should cross the Adour. I found the pontoons collected at Garris, and they were moved forward on the following days to and across the Gave de Mauleon, and the troops of the centre of the

61

army arrived.

On the 24th, Lieut.-General Sir R. Hill passed the Gave d'Oleron at Villenave, with the light, 2nd, and Portuguese divisions, under the command of Major-General Baron C. Alten, Lieut.-General Sir W. Stewart and Mariscal de Campo Le Cor; while Lieut.-General Sir H. Clinton passed with the 6th division between Monfort and Laas; and Lieut.-General Sir T. Picton made demonstrations, with the 3rd division, of an intention to attack the enemy's position at the bridge of Sauveterre, which induced the enemy to blow up the bridge.

Mariscal de Campo Don P. Morillo drove in the enemy's posts near Navarreins, and blockaded that place.

Marshal Sir W. Beresford likewise, who, since the movement of Sir R. Hill, on the 14th and 15th, had remained with the 4th and 7th divisions, and Colonel Vivian's brigade, in observation on the Lower Bidouze, attacked the enemy on the 23rd in their fortified posts at Hastingues and Oeyregave, on the left of the Gave de Pau, and obliged them to retire within the *tête de pont* at Peyrehorade.

Immediately after the passage of the Gave d'Oleron was effected, Sir R. Hill and Sir H. Clinton moved towards Orthez and the great road leading from Sauveterre to that town; and the enemy retired in the night from Sauveterre across the Gave de Pan, and assembled their army near Orthez on the 25th, having destroyed all the bridges on the river.

The right and right of the centre of the army assembled opposite Orthez, Lieut.-General Sir S. Cotton, with Lord E. Somerset's brigade of cavalry, and the 3rd division, under Lieut.-General Sir T. Picton, were near the destroyed ridge of Berenx; and Field-Marshal Sir W. Beresford, with the 4th and 7th divisions, under Lieut.-General Sir L. Cole and Major-General Walker, and Colonel Vivian's brigade, towards the junction of the Gave de Pau with the Gave d'Oleron.

The troops opposed to the marshal having moved on the

BATTLE OF ORTHEZ
Feb. 27th. 1814.

■ Allies   ⊡ French

25th, he crossed the Gave de Pau below the junction of the Gave d'Oleron, on the morning of the 26th, and moved along the high-road from Peyrehorade towards Orthez, on the enemy's right. As he approached General Sir S. Clinton crossed with the cavalry, and Lieut.-General Sir T. Picton, with the 3rd division below the bridge of Berenx; and I moved the 6th and light divisions to the same point; and Lieut.-General Sir R. Hill occupied the heights opposite Orthez and the high-road leading to Sauveterre.

The 6th and light divisions crossed in the morning of the 27th, at daybreak, and we found the enemy in a strong position near Orthez, with his right on a height on the highroad to Dax, and occupying the village of St. Boés, and his left on the heights above Orthez and that town, and opposing the passage of the river by Sir R. Hill.

The course of the heights on which the enemy had placed his army necessarily retired his centre, while the strength of the position gave extraordinary advantages to the flanks. I ordered Marshal Sir W. Beresford to turn and attack the enemy's right with the 4th division under Lieut.-General Sir L. Cole, and the 7th division under Major-General Walker, and Colonel Vivian's brigade of cavalry; while Lieut.-General Sir T. Picton would move along the great road leading from Peyrehorade to Orthez, and attack the heights on which the enemy's centre and left stood, with the 3rd and 6th divisions under Lieut.-General Sir H. Clinton, supported by Sir S. Cotton, with Lord E. Somerset's brigade of cavalry. Major-General Baron C. Alten with the light division, kept the communication, and was in reserve between these two attacks. I likewise desired Lieut.-General Sir R. Hill to cross the Gave, and to turn and attack the enemy's left.

Marshal Sir W. Beresford carried the village of St. Boés with the 4th division, under the command of Lieut.-General Sir L. Cole, after an obstinate resistance by the enemy; but the ground was so narrow that the troops could not deploy to attack the heights notwithstanding the repeated

Battle of Orthez February 27th, 1814

attempts of Major-General Ross and Brigadier-General Vasconcellos' Portuguese brigade; and it was impossible to turn them by the enemy's right without an excessive extension of our line. I therefore so far altered the plan of the action as to order the immediate advance of the 3rd and 6th divisions, and I moved forward Colonel Barnard's brigade of the light division to attack the left of the height on which the enemy's right stood.

This attack, led by the 52nd regiment under Lieut.-Colonel Colborne, and supported on their right by Major-General Brisbane's and Colonel Keane's brigades of the 3rd division, and by simultaneous attacks on the left by MajorGeneral Anson's brigade of the 4th division, and on the right by Lieut.-General Sir T. Picton, with the remainder of the 3rd division and the 6th division, under Lieut.-General Sir H. Clinton, dislodged the enemy from the heights and gave us the victory.

In the meantime, Lieut.-General Sir R. Hill had forced the passage of the Gave above Orthez, and seeing the state of the action, he moved immediately with the 2nd division of infantry, under Lieut.-General Sir W. Stewart, and MajorGeneral Fane's brigade of cavalry, direct for the great road from Orthez to St. Sever, thus keeping upon the enemy's left.

The enemy retired at first in admirable order, taking every advantage of the numerous good positions which the country afforded them. The losses, however, which he sustained in the continued attacks of our troops, and the danger with which he was threatened by Lieut.-General Sir R. Hill's movements, soon accelerated his movements, and the retreat at last became a flight, and the troops were in the utmost confusion.

Lieut.-General Sir S. Cotton took advantage of the only opportunity which offered to charge with Major-General Lord E. Somerset's brigade, in the neighbourhood of Sault de Navailles, where the enemy had been driven from the high-road by Lieut.-General Sir R. Hill. The 7th Hussars

Battle of Orthez.

Retreat of Soult,
to Aire.
1814

distinguished themselves upon this occasion and made many prisoners.

We continued the pursuit till it was dusk, and I halted the army in the neighbourhood of Sault de Navailles. I cannot estimate the extent of the enemy's loss; we have taken six pieces of cannon and a great many prisoners, the number I cannot at present report. The whole country is covered with their dead. The army was in the utmost confusion when I saw it passing the heights near Sault de Navailles, and many soldiers had thrown away their arms. The desertion has since been immense.

We followed the enemy on the following day to this place, and we this day passed the Adour. Marshal Sir W. Beresford marched with the light division and General Vivian's brigade upon Mont de Marsan, where he has taken a very large magazine of provisions. Lieut.-General Sir R. Hill had moved upon Aire, and the advanced posts of the centre are at Cazeres.

The enemy are apparently retiring upon Agen, and have left open the direct road towards Bordeaux.

While the operations of which I have given the report were carrying on on the right of the army, Lieut.-General Sir J. Hope, in concert with Rear-Admiral Penrose, availed himself of an opportunity which offered on the 23rd February to cross the Adour below Bayonne, and to take possession of both banks of the river at its mouth. The vessels destined to form the bridge could not get in till the 24th, when the difficult, and at this season of the year dangerous, operation of bringing them in was effected with a degree of gallantry and skill seldom equalled.

Lieut.-General Sir J. Hope particularly mentions Captain O'Reilly, Lieut. Cheshire, Lieut. Douglas, and Lieut. Collins, of the navy, and also Lieut. Debenham, Agent of Transports. And I am infinitely indebted to Rear-Admiral Penrose for the cordial assistance I received from him in preparing for this plan, and for that which he gave Lieut.-General Sir J. Hope in carrying it into execution.

The enemy conceiving that the means of crossing the river that Sir J. Hope had at his command, *viz.* rafts made of pontoons, had not enabled him to cross, a large force in the course of the 23rd attacked the corps which he had sent over on that evening. This corps consisted of six hundred men of the 2nd brigade of Guards under the command of Major-General the Hon. E. Stopford, who repulsed the enemy immediately. The rocket brigade was of great use on this occasion.

Three of the enemy's gunboats were destroyed this day; and a frigate lying in the Adour received considerable damage from the fire of a battery of 18-pounders, and was obliged to go higher up the river to the neighbourhood of the bridge.

Lieut.-General Sir J. Hope invested the citadel of Bayonne on the 25th; and Lieut.-General Don M. Freyre moved forward with the 4th Spanish Army, in consequence of directions which I had left for him.

On the 27th, the bridge having been completed, Lieut.-General Sir J. Hope deemed it expedient to invest the citadel of Bayonne more closely than he had done before; and he attacked the village of St. Etienne, which he carried, having taken a gun and some prisoners from the enemy, and his posts are now within nine hundred yards of the outworks of the place.

The result of the operations which I have detailed to Your Lordship is, that Bayonne, St. Jean Pied de Port, and Navarreins, are invested; and the army having passed the Adour, are in possession of all the great communications across that river, after having beaten the enemy, and taken their magazines.

I have ordered forward the Spanish troops under General Freyre, and the heavy British cavalry and artillery, and the Portuguese artillery.

Your Lordship will have observed with satisfaction the able assistance which I have received in these operations from Marshal Sir W. Beresford, Lieut.-Generals Sir R. Hill,

Sir J. Hope, and Sir S. Cotton; and from all the general officers and troops acting under their orders respectively. It is impossible for me sufficiently to express my sense of their merits, or of the degrees in which the country is indebted to their zeal and ability for the situation in which the army now finds itself.

All the troops distinguished themselves: the 4th division, under Lieut.-General Sir L. Cole, in the attack of St. Boés, and the subsequent endeavour to carry the heights; the 3rd, 6th, and Light Divisions, under the command of Lieut.-General Sir T. Picton, Sir H. Clinton, and Major-General C. Baron Alten, in the attack of the enemy's position on the heights, and these, and the 7th division, under Major-General Walker, in the various operations and attacks on the enemy's retreat. The charge made by the 7th Hussars under Lord E. Somerset was highly meritorious. The conduct of the artillery throughout the day deserved my highest approbation.

I am likewise much indebted to the Quartermaster-General Sir G. Murray, and the Adjutant-General Sir E. Pakenham, for the assistance I have received from them, and the officers of my personal staff; and to the Mariscal de Campo Don M. de Alava.

I must include a translation of the Belgian General A. Brialmont's very able comparison between Napoleon and Wellington. Brialmont wrote in 1857, five years after the death of Wellington, as follows:—

It is certain that in regard to genius for war, Wellington was inferior to Napoleon—the greatest general probably who ever lived. His conceptions were not so vast and not so rapid. He elaborated plans of campaign slowly and with difficulty. Bonaparte, on the other hand, almost improvised his plans and with the confidence of a man who believes in his star.

In action he had always qualities of vigour and prompt decision, which Wellington only displayed occasionally. But on the field of battle the English general was as skilful as and perhaps more skilful than the emperor. He possessed in a high degree the prompt *coup d'oeil* and ease in moving masses of men which distinguish eminent tacticians. Salamanca, Orthez, and Waterloo can be compared with the finest tactics of the Revolution and Empire.

As a strategist Napoleon is without a rival. After him, but with considerable intervals, come Prince Charles of Austria and Wellington. Both of these have given clear proof of their talents; they have combined their operations with much intelligence; but we must remember that they followed Napoleon, and naturally profited by the admirable lessons and glorious examples of the master.

It was not alone the gigantic vigour with which the Duke of Wellington resisted the fierceness of France and sustained the weakness of three inefficient cabinets that delivered the Peninsula. It was also the might and majesty with which the British soldier fought that delivered the Peninsula, and was the cause and continuance of the long drain of that Spanish ulcer which ruined Napoleon and removed from the British Empire that heavy cloud which for twenty-two years was as the shadow of its death over our realm.

Yet our soldiers fought under the dismal discouragement of official chicanery and discouragement, and the indifference, as Napier says, of a selfish aristocracy. But the lustre of our arms was a silver lining to a darksome cloud. The skilful and eloquent French officer and author who covered the retreat from Salamanca and ably evaded the disaster of Vittoria, thus wrote in 1827. I fear my translation does not do justice to this immortal tribute to the worth of our soldiers.

FOY ON BRITISH SOLDIERS.

We have seen the sons of Albion in battalion squares in the plain between the wood of Hougoumont and the village of Mont Saint Jean. In order to maintain their compact formation, they had doubled and refilled their ranks again and again. The cavalry which supported them was cut to pieces, the artillery ceased to fire; their generals and staff officers galloped hither and thither, uncertain in what square safety could be found. Waggons, wounded, reserve parts, allies streamed away in flight towards Brussels. Death was before them and busy in their ranks, disgrace was behind. In that terrible crisis the bullets of the Imperial Guards shot into their very faces, and the victorious and brilliant cavalry of France could not overcome the firmness of the British infantry.

We were tempted to believe that it had taken root in the soil, if these very battalions had not majestically moved forward a few minutes after sunset. Then the arrival of the Prussian Army disclosed to Wellington that, thanks to his numbers, thanks to their immobility, and as a reward for his skill in setting his courageous troops in battle array, he had just won the most decisive victory of our time.

But the high qualities thus displayed at Waterloo were characteristic of the British Army all through the Peninsular War.

# CHAPTER 4

# Toulouse

After the Battle of Orthez, Beresford, with the 4th and the 7th divisions, set out from the main army on the 8th March, and after crossing the wild and heathy *landes*, arrived before Bordeaux on the 12th.

I pass over the Royalist and other intrigues at this town which excite the contempt of French writers. We admire the devotion of loyalists like the Marquis de la Rochejaquelin, but Wellington lived to acknowledge that neither the British nor the French could gain much by the triumph of the old Bourbon rulers of France, and, indeed, both families were restored to the throne and ejected therefrom before Wellington's death in 1852.

The detachments at Bayonne and Bordeaux reduced the allied army almost to the level of Soult's forces. The French concentrated in March between Pau and Aire, and intended to fall on the British divisions on the left of the Adour; but Wellington, after some cavalry skirmishes near Aire, got together enough troops to withstand the irruption, and the French marshal resolved to retire to Toulouse. But his rear-guard, under Harispe and Villatte, was nearly overwhelmed by the pursuing British Light and 6th Divisions, and hussars at Tarbes.

Soult arranged his army in position before Toulouse on the 25th March. Wellington was on the Touch River in front of Toulouse till the 27th March, and he was in much doubt as to the result of this movement, as Suchet was at last induced to co-operate with Soult, and was advancing in the direction of Toulouse from Catalonia.

I venture to suggest that Soult's movement from Bayonne eastward into a difficult country, instead of retreating north, was a very able movement, especially as he drew near to Suchet, and also led Wellington far away from his ships. Had the war been prolonged, the British position, after the Battle of Toulouse, would have been very complicated.

These retreats to the flanks of the enemy's line of advance, and in such a fashion as to draw him off his intended line of operations, are highly meritorious. Such was Benedek's retreat after Königgratz to Olmutz instead of to Vienna; such, in a lesser degree and smaller scale, was Jackson's retreat to Elk Run after Kernstown, 1862; such was Chanzy's brilliant retreat to Vendôme and Le Mans in 1871. Suppose MacMahon had retreated in a similar manner to Langres and Besançon, instead of to Chalons after Woerth, what might have been the consequences?

On several occasions, lately, I have had occasion to speak in public, and to write about our cavalry, and I had the great honour of being at General Byng's cavalry manoeuvres in Sussex in 1906, and at General Rimington's in Ireland in 1905. Hence, I think I may be permitted to quote our able adversary, Foy, on the qualities of Cavalry officers (*Guerre de la Peninsula*, vol. 1).

### CAVALRY OFFICERS.

Cavalry officers of the type of Ney, who was one of the best cavalry officers of France before he displayed his talents on a wider sphere, and of Richepanse, were widely distributed in the Armies of the Republic. And we have seen, in the same year, at the head of the squadrons of the empire, Murat, Lassalle, Kellerman, Montbrun, and other very able men, skilled in the art of starting and directing the terrible tempests of cavalry *procella equestris*—to use the fine phrase of Scripture. (*Lassalle, the Hussar General* by John H. Lewis is also published by Leonaur.)

After the qualities necessary for a commander-in-chief the most sublime talent in war is that of a general of cavalry. Even if you possess the most rapid *coup d'oeil* and vigour of resolution more sudden than a racer at a gallop, it is nothing if you have not the vigour of youth, good eyes, a resounding voice, the strength of an athlete, and the agility of a centaur. Above all, it is necessary that Heaven should have lavishly endowed you with that precious gift which nothing can replace, and of which it is not so liberal as is commonly supposed—bravery.

But let not Britons ignore the splendid exploits of their own army. Before its career is closed by national apathy and party intrigue, I must quote one of our best historians on the final strategy of the Peninsular War. Alison says:—

Thus, within six weeks after the campaign of 1814 opened, Wellington had driven the French from the neighbourhood of Bayonne to Toulouse, a distance of 200 miles; had conquered the whole country between the Pyrenees and the Garonne, had passed six large and several smaller rivers, driven the enemy's forces from two fortified *têtes de pont* and many minor field works, defeated them in two pitched battles, besides several minor combats, crossed the raging flood of the Adour in the face of the garrison of Bayonne below that fortress, and laid siege to it as well as to St. Jean Pied de Port and Navarreins, and finally brought about a revolution at Bordeaux, and a declaration in favour of the Bourbon dynasty in the third city of the empire.

The Battle of Toulouse was fought three days after the fall of Napoleon, by the banks of the Seine, and yet so slow was the flight of information in those days that neither Soult nor Wellington knew of the capitulation of Fontainebleau, and hence a terrible combat by the banks of the Garonne, and both sides claimed the victory. But as Wellington said, "Marshal Soult wanted to keep me out of Toulouse, and I got in." And into further argument as to the balance of tactical advantages he refused to be drawn.

The Battle of Toulouse is a very important and instructive event of our history, and it is with the entire approval of our military authorities that I make a final obtrusion on the exceed-

**Battle of TOULOUSE.**

3RD. DIVISION

BOCK'S CAVALRY

LIGHT DIVISION

Croix d'arade

PONSONBY'S CAVALRY

SPANIARDS

Minimes

Pujade Hill

Montblanc

Sluice

Sluice

Hollow Road

Matabiau

Périole 4TH DIV.

Jumeau

Canal

HUSSARS

R. Ers

Great Redoubt

GENERAL

MARANSIN'S AND BRIGADE

D'ARNAGNAC

Calvin

Combette

St. Cyprien

St. Etienne
Sacarin

Luroux Road, Balma

VIAL

MILLS

Gaillomerie

St.
Michel

CORPS

Garonne R.

Cambon

St. Sypière

Bordes

Pont
Demoisselles

From Castlenaudary

Pech David

From Montaudran

VIVIAN'S HUSSARS

MARCH OF VIVIAN'S HUSSARS

N

Allies    French

ing great kindness of Mr. John Murray, and quote Wellington's despatches relating to this phase of the war.

To Earl Bathurst.

7th April, 1814.

Adverting to the state in which this army took the field in May last, to the number of actions in which it has been engaged, and to the small reinforcements it has received, it is a matter of astonishment that it should now be so strong. But there are limits to the numbers with which it can contend; and I am convinced Your Lordship would not wish to see the safety and honour of this handful of brave men depend upon the doubtful exertions and discipline of an undue proportion of Spanish troops.

I draw Your Lordship's attention particularly to this subject from observing in the newspapers that not only the militia battalions had been sent to Holland, as announced by Your Lordship, but that battalions of detachments had been formed of the recruits belonging to regiments in this army, and were likewise destined for the same service.

The service in Holland may doubtless be more important in the national interest than that in this country; but I hope it will be considered that that which is most important of all is, not to lose the brave army which has struggled through its difficulties for nearly six years.

To the Same.

Toulouse, 12th April, 1814.

I have the pleasure to inform Your Lordship that I entered this town this morning, which the enemy evacuated during the night, retiring by the road of Carcassone.

The continued fall of rain and the state of the river prevented me from laying the bridge till the morning of the 8th, when the Spanish corps and the Portuguese artillery, under the immediate orders of Lieut.-General Don M. Freyre, and the headquarters, crossed the Garonne.

We immediately moved forward to the neighbourhood of the town, and the 18th Hussars, under the immedi-

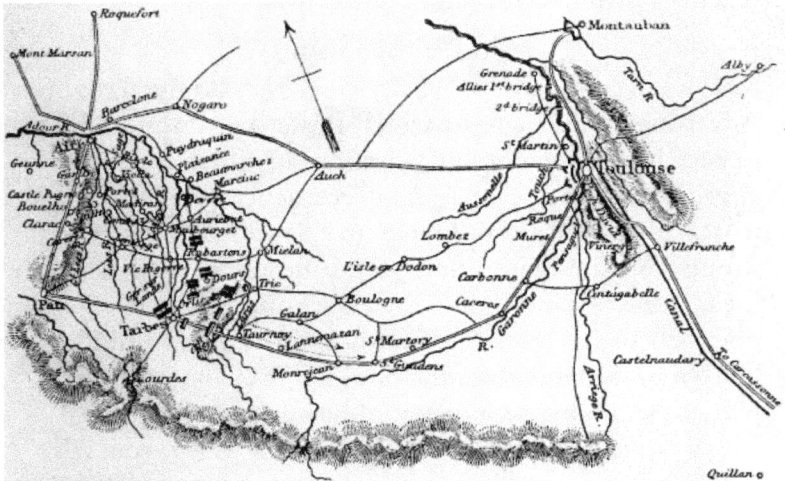

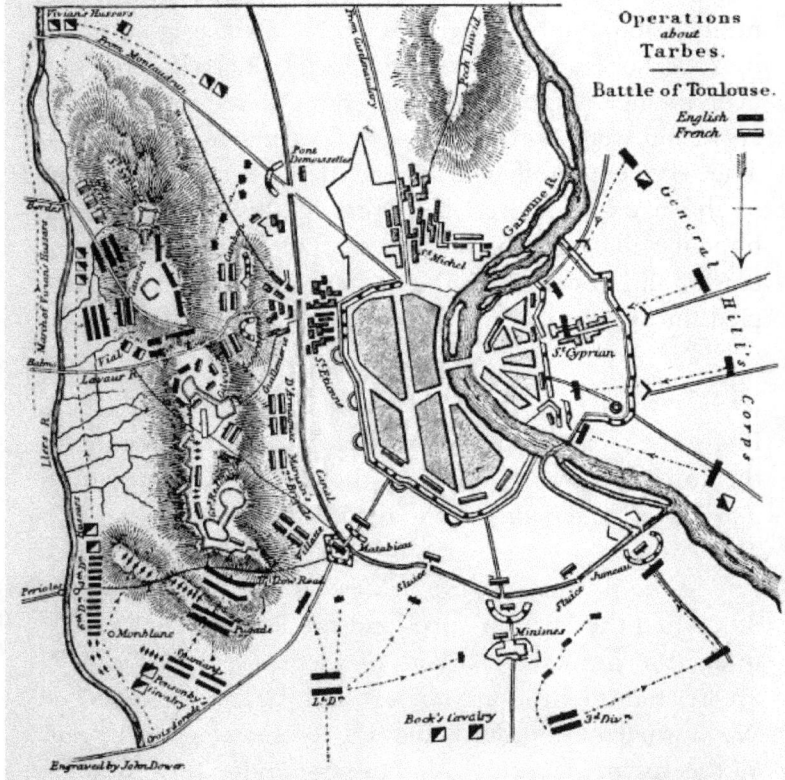

Operations
about
Tarbes.

Battle of Toulouse.

English
French

Engraved by John Dower.

ate command of Colonel Vivian, had an opportunity of making a most gallant attack upon a superior body of the enemy's cavalry, which they drove through the village of Croix d'Orade, and took about 100 prisoners, and gave us possession of an important bridge over the River Ers, by which it was necessary to pass in order to attack the enemy's position. Colonel Vivian was unfortunately wounded upon this occasion, and I am afraid I shall lose the benefit of his assistance for some time.

The town of Toulouse is surrounded on three sides by the canal of Languedoc and the Garonne. On the left of the river the suburb, which the enemy had fortified with strong field works in front of the ancient wall, formed a good *tête de pont*. They had likewise formed a *tête de pont* at each bridge of the canal, which was besides defended by the fire in some places of musketry, and in all of artillery from the ancient wall of the town.

Beyond the canal to the eastward, and between that and the River Ers, is a height which extends as far as Montaudran, and over which pass all the approaches to the canal and town to the eastward, which it defends; and the enemy, in addition to the *têtes de pont* on the bridges of the canal, had fortified this height with five redoubts, connected by lines of entrenchments, and had, with extraordinary diligence, made every preparation for defence. They had likewise broken all the bridges over the Ers within our reach, by which the right of the position could be approached. The roads, however, from the Arriège to Toulouse being impracticable for cavalry or artillery, and nearly so for infantry, as reported in my despatch to Your Lordship of the 1st inst., I had no alternative, excepting to attack the enemy in this formidable position.

It was necessary to move the pontoon bridge higher up the Garonne, in order to shorten the communication with Lieut.-General Sir R. Hill's corps, as soon as the Spanish corps had passed; and this operation was not effected till so late an hour on the 9th as to induce me to defer the attack till the following morning.

The plan, according to which I determined to attack the enemy, was for Marshal Sir W. Beresford, who was on the right of the Ers with the 4th and 6th divisions, to cross that river at the bridge of Croix d'Orade, to gain possession of Montblanc, and to march up the left of the Ers to turn the enemy's right, while Lieut.-General Don M. Freyre, with the Spanish corps under his command, supported by the British cavalry, should attack the front. Lieut.-General Sir S. Cotton was to follow the marshal's movement with Major-General Lord E. Somerset's brigade of hussars; and Colonel Vivian's brigade, under the command of Colonel Arenschilt, was to observe the movements of the enemy's cavalry on both banks of the Ers beyond our left.

The 3rd and Light Divisions, under the command of General Sir T. Picton and Major-General C. Baron Alten, and the brigade of German cavalry, were to observe the enemy on the lower part of the canal, and to draw their attention to that quarter by threatening the *têtes de pont*, while Lieut.-General Sir R. Hill was to do the same on the suburb on the left of the Garonne.

Marshal Sir W. Beresford crossed the Ers, and formed his corps in three columns of lines in the village of Croix d'Orade, the 4th division leading, with which he immediately carried Montblanc. He then moved up the Ers in the same order over most difficult ground in a direction parallel to the enemy's fortified position; and as soon as he reached the point at which he turned it, he formed his lines and moved to the attack. During these operations Lieut.-General Don M. Freyre moved along the left of the Ers to the front of Croix d'Orade, where he formed his corps in two lines with a reserve on a height in front of the enemy's position, on which height the Portuguese artillery were placed; and Major-General Ponsonby's brigade of cavalry in reserve in the rear.

As soon as formed, and that it was seen that Marshal Sir W. Beresford was ready, Lieut.-General Don M. Freyre

BATTLE OF TOULOUSE APRIL 10TH, 1814

moved forward to the attack. The troops marched in good order, under a very heavy fire of musketry and artillery, and showed great spirit, the general and all his Staff being at their head; and the two lines were soon lodged under some banks immediately under the enemy's entrenchments, the reserve and Portuguese artillery and British cavalry continuing on the height on which the troops had first formed.

The enemy, however, repulsed the movement of the right of General Freyre's line round their left flank, and having followed up their success, and turned our right by both sides of the high-road leading from Toulouse to Croix d'Orade, they soon compelled the whole corps to retire. It gave me great satisfaction to see that, although they suffered considerably in retiring, the troops rallied again as soon as the Light Division, which was immediately on their right, moved up; and I cannot sufficiently applaud the exertions of Lieut.-General Don M. Freyre, the officers of the staff of the 4th Spanish Army, and of the officers of the general staff, to rally and form them again.

Lieut.-General Mendizabel, who was in the field as a volunteer. General Ezpeleta, and several officers and chiefs of corps, were wounded upon this occasion; but General Mendizabel continued in the field. The regiment of *Tiradores de Cantabria*, under the command of Colonel Leon de Sicilia, kept its position, under the enemy's entrenchments, until I ordered it to retire.

In the meantime, Marshal Sir W. Beresford, with the 4th division under the command of Lieut.-General Sir L. Cole, and the 6th division under the command of Lieut.-General Sir H. Clinton, attacked and carried the heights on the enemy's right, and the redoubt which covered and protected that flank; and he lodged these troops on the same height with the enemy, who were, however, still in possession of four redoubts, and of the entrenchments and fortified houses.

The badness of the roads had induced the marshal to

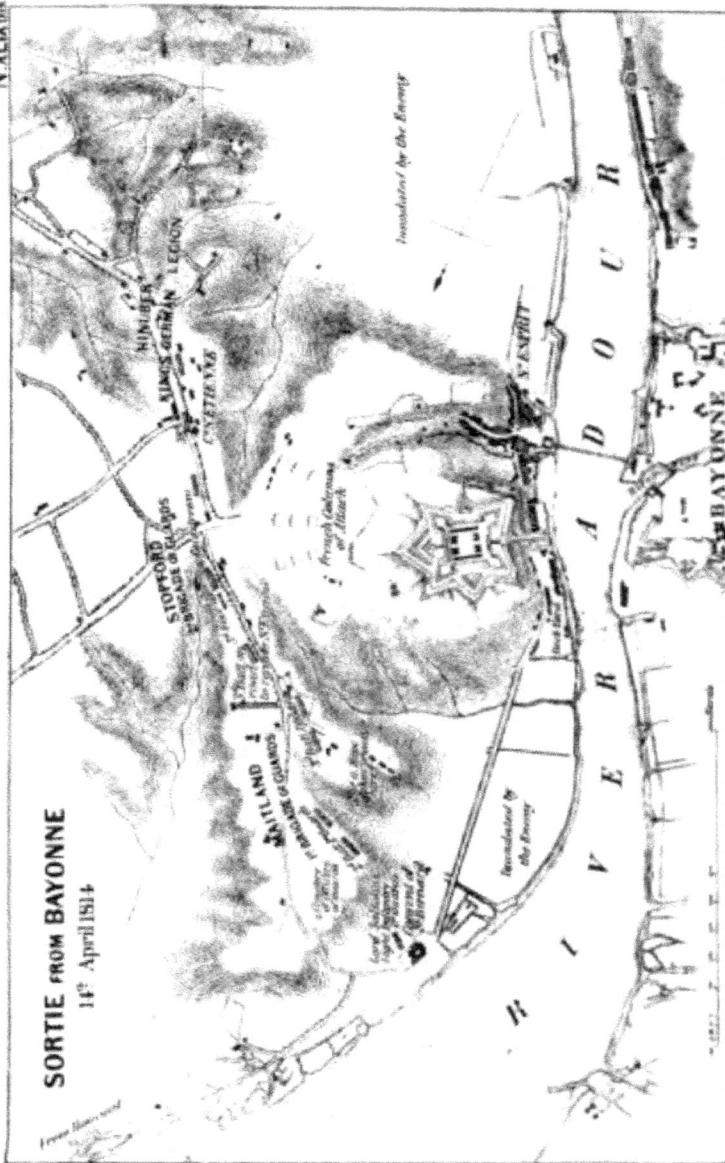

SORTIE FROM BAYONNE
14° April 1814

leave his artillery in the village of Montblanc; and some time elapsed before it could be brought to him, and before Lieut.-General Don M. Freyre's corps could be re-formed and brought back to the attack. As soon as this was effected, the marshal continued his movement along the ridge, and carried, with General Pack's brigade of the 6th division, the two principal redoubts and fortified houses in the enemy's centre.

The enemy made a desperate effort from the canal to re-gain these redoubts, but they were repulsed with consid-erable loss; and the 6th division continuing its movements along the ridge of the height, and the Spanish troops con-tinuing a corresponding movement upon the front, the enemy were driven from the two redoubts and entrench-ments on the left, and the whole range of heights were in our possession.

We did not gain this advantage, however, without severe loss; particularly in the brave 6th division. Lieut.-Colonel Coghlan of the 61st, an officer of great merit and prom-ise, was unfortunately killed in the attack of the heights. Major-General Pack was wounded, but was enabled to remain in the field; and Colonel Douglas, of the 8th Por-tuguese regiment, lost his leg, and I am afraid that I shall be deprived for a considerable time of his assistance.

The 36th, 42nd, 79th, and 61st lost considerable numbers, and were highly distinguished throughout the day.

I cannot sufficiently applaud the ability and conduct of Marshal Sir W. Beresford throughout the operations of the day; nor that of Lieut.-Generals Sir L. Cole, Sir H. Clinton, Major-Generals Pack and Lambert, and the troops under their command. Marshal Sir W. Beresford particularly re-ports the good conduct of Brigadier-General d'Urban, the quartermaster-general, and General Brito Mozinho, the adjutant-general to the Portuguese Army.

The 4th division, though much exposed on their march along the enemy's front to a galling fire, were not so much engaged as the 6th, and did not suffer so much; but they

THE SORTIE FROM BAYONNE, AT 3 IN THE MORNING, ON THE 14TH OF APRIL, 1914

conducted themselves with their usual gallantry.

I had also every reason to be satisfied with the conduct of Lieut.-General Don M. Freyre, Lieut.-General Don G. Mendizabel, Marisco de Campo Don P. Barcenas, Brigadier Don J. de Ezpeleta, Mariscal de Campo Don A. Garces de Marcilla, and the chief of the staff, Don E. S. Salvado, and the officers of the staff of the 4th army. The officers and troops conducted themselves well in all the attacks which they made subsequent to their being re-formed.

The ground not having admitted of the operations of the cavalry, they had no opportunity of charging.

While the operations above detailed were going on on the left of the army, Lieut.-General Sir R. Hill drove the enemy from their exterior works in the suburb, on the left of the Garonne, within the ancient wall. Lieut.-General Sir T. Picton likewise, with the 3rd division, drove the enemy within the *tête de pont* on the bridge of the canal nearest the Garonne; but the troops having made an effort to carry it, they were repulsed, and some loss was sustained. Major-General Brisbane was wounded; but I hope not so as to deprive me for any length of time of his assistance; and Lieut.-Colonel Forbes of the 45th, an officer of great merit, was killed.

The army being thus established on three sides of Toulouse, I immediately detached our light cavalry to cut off the communication by the only road practicable for carriages which remained to the enemy, till I should be enabled to make arrangements to establish the troops between the canal and the Garonne.

The enemy, however, retired last night, leaving in our hands General Harispe, General Baurot, General St. Hilaire, and 1,600 prisoners. One piece of cannon was taken on the field of battle; and others, and large quantities of stores of all descriptions, in the town.

Since I sent my last report, I have received an account from Rear-Admiral Penrose of the successes in the Gironde of the boats of the squadron under his command.

Lieut.-General the Earl of Dalhousie crossed the Garonne nearly about the time that Admiral Penrose entered the river, and pushed the enemy's parties under General L'Huillier beyond the Dordogne. He then crossed the Dordogne on the 4th, near St. Andre de Cubsac, with a detachment of the troops under his command, with a view to the attack of the fort of Blaye. His lordship found General L'Huillier and General Desbareaux posted near Etauliers, and made his disposition to attack them, when they retired, leaving about 300 prisoners in his hands. I enclose the Earl of Dalhousie's report of this affair.

In the operations which I have now reported, I have had every reason to be satisfied with the assistance I received from the quartermaster and adjutant-general, and officers of those departments respectively; from Mariscal de Campo Don L. Wimpffen and the officers of the Spanish Staff, and from Mariscal de Campo Don M. de Alava; from Colonel Dickson, commanding the allied artillery, and from Lieut.-Colonel Lord Fitzroy Somerset and the officers of my personal staff.

# Conclusion

At present the international condition of the world is far more threatening to the future of the British Empire than were all the energy and skill of Napoleon and his marshals. From Trafalgar, 1805, to Toulouse, 1814, no combination of all the navies in the world could restrain our commerce or interrupt the communications of our army, and we could threaten with impunity every port from St. Petersburg to Cadiz, and thence to the Dardanelles, and land expeditionary forces at the mouth of the Potomac, at Buenos Ayres, in Denmark, Egypt, at the Cape of Good Hope, and we controlled every archipelago from Corfu to Java. Now we are by no means the only naval power, and we must count upon the influence in international strategy of the yellow race as well as of Europe and of the United States, and yet we do not take half as effective precautions to secure military success as our ancestors took at three times the pressure on their means, in 1808.

If an over-sea campaign was necessary tomorrow, we would not be ready in any sense. In every way our army is inferior absolutely and relatively to its condition in 1808-1814. Napier fiercely attacked sophists and mere rhetoricians and economists and party charlatans in his time. What would he say were he living now, when temporising and extemporising partisans are mere resonators for wire-pulling chicanery, and the reduction of our forces is supposed to be a way of increasing their strength? But let "paltry pedants prattle as they will," a nation that forgets the lessons of war is ignoring the happiness of its posterity.

Yet I trust that I have proved that Britons may well rejoice in the glory of their arms. It is a stirring sound. They did nobly in war, whether they started from Inverness, or Cardiff, or York, or London, or Galway, or Cork, to bear the Union Jack from the Tagus to the Douro and the Ebro, and over the defiles once traversed by Charlemagne and his *paladins*.

Fuentarabia and Roncesvaux re-echoed the strains of the fifes of the English grenadiers descending the Pyrenees. "Wild and high the Cameron's gathering rose, the pibroch of Lochiel," not now in Caledonia, but where the strong fortresses of Soult seemed to render impassable the passages of the Bidassoa and the Nivelle. Nor were the Irish Celts untrue to Scotch and Saxon comrades, the wild cry of Faugh-a-Ballaugh was a prelude to a wilder rush at Barossa, against the astonished veterans of Marshal Victor.

Alas! that such memories should be the sport of blatant impostors even as beautiful leaves are wasted by crawling caterpillars; but as Napier says:

The noblest dwellings are often defiled by foul and creeping things.

War is, on the whole, not only a great and glorious thing, but it is the necessary condition of the world. From insects to animals all are at strife—but the glory of arms, which cannot be obtained without the exercise of honour, fortitude, courage, obedience, modesty, and temperance, excites the poor man's patriotism, and is a chastening corrective for the rich man's pride.

No Hague Conference will stop the current of humanity. If Europe disarmed, Asia would arm, and the doctrines of Islam and Buddhism would soon be preached in St. Peter's, and Notre Dame, and St. Paul's. Without war there would be no Christianity, no manhood, no virtue. Without the cult of chivalry and valour the English would now be a lower race than were the Chinese in 1890. Without war the human soul would have been "potted" in America in 1863. The arts of war never ruined any nation; the arts of peace and the evil devices of faction, and luxury, and sports, and party have ruined many nations, and are ruining the English.

LEONAUR

# ALSO FROM LEONAUR
## AVAILABLE IN SOFTCOVER OR HARDCOVER WITH DUST JACKET

**A DIARY FROM DIXIE** *by Mary Boykin Chesnut*—A Lady's Account of the Confederacy During the American Civil War

**FOLLOWING THE DRUM** *by Teresa Griffin Vielé*—A U. S. Infantry Officer's Wife on the Texas frontier in the Early 1850's

**FOLLOWING THE GUIDON** *by Elizabeth B. Custer*—The Experiences of General Custer's Wife with the U. S. 7th Cavalry.

**LADIES OF LUCKNOW** *by G. Harris & Adelaide Case*—The Experiences of Two British Women During the Indian Mutiny 1857. A Lady's Diary of the Siege of Lucknow by G. Harris, Day by Day at Lucknow by Adelaide Case

**MARIE-LOUISE AND THE INVASION OF 1814** *by Imbert de Saint-Amand*— The Empress and the Fall of the First Empire

**SAPPER DOROTHY** *by Dorothy Lawrence*—The only English Woman Soldier in the Royal Engineers 51st Division, 79th Tunnelling Co. during the First World War

**ARMY LETTERS FROM AN OFFICER'S WIFE 1871-1888** *by Frances M. A. Roe*—Experiences On the Western Frontier With the United States Army

**NAPOLEON'S LETTERS TO JOSEPHINE** *by Henry Foljambe Hall*—Correspondence of War, Politics, Family and Love 1796-1814

**MEMOIRS OF SARAH DUCHESS OF MARLBOROUGH, AND OF THE COURT OF QUEEN ANNE VOLUME 1** by A. T. Thomson

**MEMOIRS OF SARAH DUCHESS OF MARLBOROUGH, AND OF THE COURT OF QUEEN ANNE VOLUME 2** by A. T. Thomson

**MARY PORTER GAMEWELL AND THE SIEGE OF PEKING** *by A. H. Tuttle*—An American Lady's Experiences of the Boxer Uprising, China 1900

**VANISHING ARIZONA** *by Martha Summerhayes*—A young wife of an officer of the U.S. 8th Infantry in Apacheria during the 1870's

**THE RIFLEMAN'S WIFE** *by Mrs. Fitz Maurice*—*The Experiences of an Officer's Wife and Chronicles of the Old 95th During the Napoleonic Wars*

**THE OATMAN GIRLS** *by Royal B. Stratton*—The Capture & Captivity of Two Young American Women in the 1850's by the Apache Indians

www.ingramcontent.com/pod-product-compliance
Lightning Source LLC
Chambersburg PA
CBHW032023090426
42741CB00006B/718